LARRY CULLIFORD

W0193414

THE BIG BOOK OF
WISDOM

WHAT IS WISDOM?
WHY WE NEED IT
HOW TO GET IT.

Endorsements for
The Big Book of Wisdom

'In our time of disorientation and disconnection from our roots, Larry Culliford gives us the benefit of his wise and compassionate insights into the life journey we all share, and helpful signposts along the path to genuine responsibility and spiritual maturity. This gem of a book engages readers in an open and accessible way with the essentials of life and the challenges of living, growing, healing and ultimately surrendering all our attachments. Larry invites us to be drawn into a seamless connection to the whole, which is a critical message at every level.'

David Lorimer, Programme Director, Scientific and Medical Network

'It is welcome to have a modern reflection of how people today might find wisdom. With his experience as a psychiatrist and his ability to embrace the Christian and other spiritual traditions, Larry Culliford examines how people mature and how healthy maturity leads to wisdom. This skilful author shows himself as a wise teacher whose wisdom needs to be heard.'

Dominic Walker OGS, former Bishop of Monmouth

'Psychiatrist and spiritual writer Larry Culliford draws on a lifetime of serious reflection around issues of human meaning, self-understanding, and the complex, layered and protracted process of aching into holiness, of achieving a new way of seeing, sapientia. His new book is an enchiridion *or spiritual handbook for those questers keen on deepening their interiority, their spiritual maturity. An engaging read.'*

Michael W. Higgins, Ph.D., LL.D., D.H.L. Distinguished Professor of Catholic Thought, Sacred Heart University, Fairfield, CT 06825.

Hero, 51 Gower Street, London, WC1E 6HJ
hero@hero-press.com | www.hero-press.com

Contents © Larry Culliford 2020
The right of the above author to be identified as the author of this work has been asserted in accordance with the Copyright, Designs and Patents Act 1988. British Library Cataloguing in Publication Data available.

Print ISBN 978-1-78955-1-211
Ebook ISBN 978-1-78955-1-228
Set in Times. Production managed by Jellyfish Solutions Ltd.

CONTENTS

PART THREE: SEEKING WISDOM
Things you may want to do

The Big Book of Wisdom is an expanded, less politically focused version of *Seeking Wisdom – A Spiritual Manifesto*, which was first published in 2017 by Buckingham University Press. (See 'Author's Notes'.)

Original Foreword to *Seeking Wisdom*

In October 1517, Martin Luther challenged the supreme temporal and spiritual authority of his time by criticizing the mercenary priorities of the Pope and the Roman Catholic Church. His widely-disseminated Ninety-five Theses became pivotal in starting the Protestant Reformation. Powerful divisive echoes and after-shocks of that rift permeate world culture today. Now, 500 years later, comes a differently challenging document. This time the force behind it is healing, not divisive. *Seeking Wisdom* is a unifying text with, at its core, the uplifting message that, 'We are all already one'.

A lifetime writing about prime ministers and others who have reached the top of the tree in politics, business and other fields has led me to one very clear conclusion: neither age, nor power, nor charisma, nor money necessarily lead either to wisdom or happiness.

Since the office was created in 1721, Britain has seen fifty-five prime ministers. Despite having achieved the pinnacle of politics, surprisingly few were happy, nor did they develop happiness after leaving Downing Street. An even smaller number developed any measure of wisdom, perhaps five of the fifty-five, including, in the last one hundred years, and then only at the end of their careers, Winston Churchill and James Callaghan.

It is a consoling thought that power and money often lead

away from rather than towards wisdom and happiness. It is consoling, too, to understand that we can all learn to be wise regardless of our standing in life. Humility is a necessary ingredient of wisdom, so it can indeed be easier for those who have least (in worldly terms anyway) to become wise and rich in spirit. The passage from The Bible known as 'The Beatitudes' is just one religious text among many which make this abundantly clear.

In this book, the very experienced writer, psychiatrist and psychologist, Larry Culliford, offers a succinct yet profound road map for how anyone can learn to become a wiser, more mature human being. The approach applies equally to those of any religious faith and none, as long as the seeker is prepared to be open minded about spiritual progress.

The firmest believers in all religions are seldom, of course, open minded. It would be wonderful if the leaders of all nations on earth, and in all walks of life, were to read this praiseworthy volume. We cannot assume that they will. But equally we cannot discount that they might. Whether they do or not is beyond our power. What is within our power is to read and engage fully with this book ourselves, and to have our lives changed significantly for the better by doing so. Our lives will be changed but, more importantly still, so will the lives and opportunities of all those with whom we have dealings and come to influence, in this generation and in the generations to come.

Martin Luther disturbed the status quo to its core and precipitated centuries of bloody division and war. With your present mindedness, inspired I would hope by this spiritual manifesto, the reverse, a healing and homecoming process, can be initiated. In this way, little by little, the restoration of harmony – at home, in communities, and between people hitherto in conflict – can begin.

Anthony Seldon
Vice Chancellor, University of Buckingham
November 2017

From the original 'Introduction' to *Seeking Wisdom*

Recent elections and referenda have yielded unexpected results. These include the Scottish Independence and Brexit referenda, the Northern Ireland Assembly, US Presidency, and French elections, also two British General Elections. Political parties appear struggling to decide and agree on fixed aims and policies that both appeal to voters and address realistically the challenges of the times. A new degree of flexibility is required that does not fit well with the traditional structures of political life.

Voters are dealing with a greater degree of uncertainty, and a political landscape containing a plethora of powerful vested interests. Leadership that looks strong often turns out to be brittle. Flexible leadership, on the other hand, easily appears malleable and weak.

When leadership is unsatisfactory, a greater responsibility falls upon individual members of society. It becomes necessary to think matters through personally; and this manifesto is offered as a discussion document, as a broad-stroke blueprint for people seeking personal growth and wisdom in decision-making. It is not a conventional political statement, because it is not concerned with canvassing for votes in order to take control of the State. Instead of political *power*, it looks rather towards exerting wide-ranging public *influence*, focusing on informing the general way of life of citizens from all political persuasions.

Such a document, rather than a partisan rallying call, therefore offers suggestions and guidance for unification and harmony. It takes as a starting point that, moment by moment, wisdom seeks what is best for all, in any given situation. It brings people together rather than dividing them. Wisdom necessarily therefore embodies compassion – caring about people; being prepared to suffer with, and on behalf of, others.

This book, then, is a public declaration recommending a universal policy of seeking wisdom, both in private and public life, with the patient aim of nothing less than improving life quality for all.

Larry Culliford
September 2017

Brief Definitions

'Avoid wrangling over words, which does no good...'[1]

Paradigm: a way of seeing or construing the world which underlies the theories, operating principles, rules and methodologies of science during a particular period of history. It includes the values, assumptions and beliefs accepted by the scientific community of the day.

Paradigm Shift: a major change in both theory and practice that is necessarily a development of what has gone before: for example, the arrival of Einstein's relativity theory required a new way of looking at and explaining things, an expansion of the earlier physics of Isaac Newton.

Paradox: a form of truth that includes apparent contradictions, which at first glance may seem strange and unlikely. (For example, *The Big Book of Wisdom* weighs in at under a kilo, but is still 'big' on account of its all-embracing content.)

Spirit: a word, derived from the Latin *spiritus*, meaning 'breath' or 'wind', that can be used to denote 'life force' or 'cosmic energy'.

---

1. St Paul's second letter to Timothy; chapter 2, verse 14.

Spirituality: a word sometimes used to refer to human understanding and experience of 'wherever the deeply personal meets the universal'.

Holy: a word, sharing a common root with *whole* and *heal* (i.e. 'making whole'), that implies a supreme unifying principle.

Holy Spirit: is therefore a phrase that can be used to refer to a sacred, all-powerful, unifying life force, or cosmic energy.

PART ONE
EXPLANATION

Things You May Want To Know

'We are already one. But we imagine that we are not.
And what we have to recover is our original unity.
What we have to be is what we are.'

Thomas Merton [2]

2. Thomas Merton (1973) *The Asian Journal of Thomas Merton,* New York: New Directions, p 308.

1

WHAT IS WISDOM AND WHY DO WE NEED IT

Wisdom is universal. Everyone has some idea what the word means, but it is tricky to describe. Here is a brief working definition for readers to reflect on and play around with:

Wisdom is the knowledge of how to be and behave for the best, for all concerned, in any given situation.

As a form of knowledge, wisdom is different in character from scientific knowledge. Unlike the knowledge of facts, wisdom varies; what works in one situation, at this particular time, and for one person, may fail in other circumstances, at a different time, or for another person. Also, rather than being deduced by reasoned thinking, it is intuitive.

In one way, wisdom is like all true knowledge, in that it can be considered sacred. To be sacred means to be inviolable, beyond personal opinions and preferences. It also means to be full of power. In this sense, wisdom and spirituality are closely related. The search for wisdom can therefore be said to involve an improving degree of spiritual awareness. It is about a person – and, collectively, a community or society – becoming increasingly experienced in life's problems and how best to resolve them, growing in psychological and spiritual maturity.

Readers may not like to think of themselves as immature. It can feel uncomfortable, a threat to one's self-image. Nevertheless, it is important to recognise – in oneself and others – the potential for further growth and development. And it helps to realise that this is a process of nature; natural personal, psychological and spiritual evolution; also that, accordingly, it takes time.

Where does wisdom come from? It cannot be said to depend on holding any particular beliefs, whether ideological, political, religious or non-religious. It does depend, though, on having (even briefly or subliminally; that is, just at the rim of consciousness) a profound and mysterious sense of cosmic wholeness. According to such experience, a person feels wonderfully connected to the totality of the universe, to all of nature, and through this to everything and everyone else, to every other person, regardless of age, race, creed, colour, sexual preferences or anything else.

For people who have not yet had this type of exposure, or who remain sceptical about such things, it needs saying that, according to the scheme outlined later (in Chapter 3), everything and everyone – past, present and to come — are seamlessly and timelessly connected through the spiritual dimension of human experience. This indicates that what a person thinks, says and does moment by moment, has an effect – however subtle – on everyone and everything else. Wisdom, then, involves taking mature and continuing responsibility for one's thoughts, words and actions – equally and importantly, for one's silences and inaction, for what you avoid saying and do not do. This is maturity. Involving much more than intellectual understanding, wisdom is a vital part of who we are, both individually and collectively; not only of who we are, but also who we can be and are set on becoming.

It also needs saying that people need to be prepared for the idea that growth of this kind, the gaining of wisdom, involves engaging with suffering, with all the different types of pain that any person might encounter: physical, emotional, social and spiritual; from daily minor discomforts to extremes of near-intolerable distress. These pages speak not only of how to suffer less, but also of how to make the most of painful experiences, one's own and those of others. They assert that the outcome of suffering, when endured and somehow transcended, is wisdom; and this in turn involves having an increasing capacity for living calmly and joyfully, without destructive levels of painful feelings, without giving way to excessive fear, anger or sorrow. However hard won or easily come by, wisdom involves the ability to live contentedly, in an infectious manner that spontaneously informs and influences others, so that everyone benefits.

* * *

Why do we need wisdom? Firstly, everyone needs to seek and attain as great a measure of wisdom as possible for the common good. Being based on the principle of universal human connectedness, wisdom therefore directly invokes virtues like humility, tolerance, restraint, patience, gratitude, generosity, forgiveness, honesty and compassion. These attributes form the basis of social well-being. Because they are among the indicators of supreme mental health, this indicates the second reason: we need wisdom, and do well to seek it, for maximum personal benefit too.

Here is confirmation from Tibetan spiritual master, the Dalai Lama:

> *I try to promote human compassion based on a sense that all human beings are one. This way of thinking is of immense benefit to me. When I meet someone with two eyes, one nose and so forth, I recognise*

them as physically, mentally and emotionally the
same as me. I feel they are my sister or brother.[3]

Consider the alternative; that is, people behaving from principally selfish motives, seeking personal gain, intent on avoiding pain and suffering. Words denoting the opposite of wisdom, its absence, are also universally known: 'craziness', 'madness', 'stupidity', 'foolishness' or 'folly'. This kind of reversal and rejection of wisdom may be based either on blameless (but unfortunate) inexperience, or on a particularly regrettable kind of wilful ignorance, a diversion away from or active suppression of the virtues listed above. The consequences of such rejection of wisdom are everywhere, so another reason we need wisdom, and need it urgently, concerns the present state of the world. Quite literally, global affairs are growing too hot for humanity.

* * *

What follows is a necessarily brief, therefore seemingly blunt and brutal account of humanity's present troubles, doubtlessly already familiar in readers' minds. The difference here is an overview that demonstrates their inter-locking nature; that they are all attributable in this analysis to a single basic cause, one which is amenable to remedy. This description both offers hope and points to a constructive way forward. In summary, there is a widespread dearth of wisdom, and an associated, unmet hunger for spiritual energy and experience.

This exploration of the current maelstrom of human suffering begins with the huge threat to everyone that is represented by global warming. Little by little, scientists say, the planet is warming up as a result of increasing greenhouse gas emissions, due to both heavy consumption of fossil fuels,

---

3. The Dalai Lama at a Meeting with Global Youth Leaders in New Delhi on 7th April 2019, as reported in *The Tibet Foundation Newsletter*, No 74, Spring 2019, p 5.

and the mounting destruction of rain-forests, which nullifies the protective effects of trees and other vegetation. After a period of denial, which persists in some quarters, this is now given widespread credence, to the extent of a world-wide movement being founded and gaining large numbers of followers. According to the Extinction Rebellion website:

We are facing an unprecedented global emergency. Life on Earth is in crisis: scientists agree we have entered a period of abrupt climate breakdown, and we are in the midst of a mass extinction of our own making. [4]

But this is only a starting point. Because many aspects of human suffering can be linked to the same set of causes, wisdom involves having very broad vision, seeing connections between things and having a full grasp of their context. Only then is it possible to see clearly how almost all the major problems that worry people intensely are closely inter-related.

Global warming, fuel-burning and eco-destruction are strongly associated with the prevalent science-dominated techno-culture at the heart of which is an immature attitude, a kind of hubris, an excessive and presumptuous self-confidence that was perfectly understandable in the middle years of the last century when astonishing progress in disease control, family planning, transportation, computing and information technology, space exploration and much more, strengthened the idea that the world belonged to humankind to exploit, plunder at will and control.

Alongside the resulting materialist industrialisation and progress came international competition for wealth, territory and resources, accompanied by the polarisation of national populations and other partisan groupings, together with a nuclear 'arms race', a 'space race', and the development of all manner of terrifyingly powerful military hardware. Division

---

4. See Appendix 2 for website details.

and competition between countries has been fuelled by the need of arms developers to sell their guns, missiles, bombs, fighter planes, drones, military computer systems and so on for maximum profit, thus continuing to tighten the spiral towards 'Mutually Assured Destruction' and beyond; and all this has ensured so far is that warfare and violence continue with an unprecedented capacity for homicidal annihilation, biological desolation and material devastation. It is as if humankind is going through a troubled and troublesome adolescence, with people tending to blame others for their miseries, and then finding or creating excuses to flex their powerful, new-found military might and muscles. It is hard to avoid feeling anxious about the situation, but wherever there is immaturity, there is also the inherent possibility of ripening to magnificent fruition.

At the personal level, from about the middle 1950s, encouraged by the wider cultural changes, more liberal attitudes, and the feelings of security that prevailed, people in many places began holding increasingly materialist ambitions; such as, to give just two examples, to drive a car and fly in a plane. With the world population stretching inexorably now towards eight thousand million people, the consequences in terms of fossil fuel consumption and atmospheric pollution are obvious. Obviously society cannot do without some form of economic exchange and commerce. This is so even in socialist and communist states. However, in the west, encouraged by profit-seeking industry, by consumerism, by advertising and the relentless imperative of growth economics, we have all been encouraged to desire and go after ever-increasing 'success' in terms of profit, property, possessions, position and power over others. This poses a threat, overturning a healthier balance between worldliness and spirituality.

It is perfectly natural and acceptable for people to want things that make life easier and more comfortable. However, there is a downside to such worldly and materialist appetites. They have a strong tendency towards the suppression of more spiritual values, those based on universal feelings of kinship. In the struggle to fulfil our desires, bent on acquiring more and more stuff and status, other people get treated as either supporters or competitors, friends or foe, which fosters a powerful propensity for creating rivals and opponents, real or imagined, threatening our precious status, wealth and well-being. *'If you're not a success, you're a failure... If not with us, you're against us!'* These immature, intolerant, destructive, die-hard formulae urgently need revision in the interests not only of social harmony but also of human survival.

Many people have already paid the price of adolescent aims and ideals like these, and millions are still doing so. War and intolerance lead not only to death and destruction of cities. They lead directly to a rise in terrorism, also to the widespread displacement of innocent people from their homes and homelands. Similarly, the climate changes accompanying global warming and the unstable weather patterns that follow have resulted in natural disasters of greater frequency and intensity, contributing significantly in turn to catastrophic famine, poverty, starvation and sickness epidemics. Who can deny that the outcome of these calamities, like that of mass violence and military activity, involves the further displacement of millions of helpless people? We see it on our television screens and find it elsewhere across the media every day.

Rich countries tend to exploit poorer countries where the people, seeing and hearing about the accompaniments of wealth and luxury elsewhere, become filled with envy and ambition; not wanting even a car or a plane flight, but hoping simply for safe drinking water, a shower and an indoor toilet. There is, then, a natural push to modernise and industrialise these less rich countries, with added consequences for fossil fuel consumption, global warming and so on. Toxic chemicals released into the environment cause havoc to wildlife in the countryside. Particulate matter pollutes the air of our cities, aggravating people's breathing difficulties, even crossing placentas into babies growing in the womb. Plastic waste is everywhere: in our precious rivers and the great oceans of the planet; in Antarctic ice, in our drinking water, and even microscopically in our own precious bodies. Furthermore, where material progress is delayed, people set off for better conditions elsewhere, in doing so joining a class of people known as 'economic migrants', a large sub-class of the already existing millions of refugees from war, genocide, natural and man-made disasters.

This all adds to the story. Like refugees, these migrants are vulnerable to sickness and malnutrition, also to merciless exploitation. Restrictions are placed on their movements by some of the more affluent countries. Impersonal, soul-sapping containment centres are built. Barriers are constructed and policed to keep them out; but still they come, flowing like rivers in flood, ill-equipped to travel but prepared to brave all dangers and hardships, separation from loved ones, repeated failure and repatriation, even unceremonious death, for example in unseaworthy craft on a perilous ocean.

The wisdom of human unity suggests that what they want is what everybody else wants too: a decent and comfortable life. More than that, in many cases they are driven by the deepest of impulses, that their lives should be meaningful and thereby productive, given in some way for the ultimate benefit of others; for their family, their friends and fellow-countrymen, their new companions and even strangers. This is a universal imperative, a spiritual drive to feel worthy among fellow citizens, to offer a contribution to society, to make a difference.

The great tragedy of so many refugees is that they do not want so much to take as to give, and give fully of themselves, but there are very limited opportunities for them to do this. They want education, and they want useful work, not only to repay what they received when they were in need, and to be able to send much-needed funds home, but also to achieve self-respect, and perhaps a position from which later they might return to their homeland with new knowledge, skills, ideas and ambitions, seeking in turn to improve the welfare of all who dwell in that place.

This is the dream of these migrants and refugees, just like the purest dreams of everyone else, which makes these unfortunate ones the spiritual brothers and sisters of those who, in wealthier situations, have the blessings of greater safety and stability. The noble aspirations they hold are born of a genuinely spiritual sensibility regarding the unity of humankind. Those who are materially better off are given a choice, whether to accept or reject these pilgrims. Many see them only as 'outsiders', as a threat, and this is part of their tragedy. To suppress the spirit of others is to do equal damage to our own.

According to the universal 'law of cause and effect' (known in the East as *'karma'*), every kind or unkind word spoken and act performed is repaid accordingly. Similarly, well-meant and deliberate silence or the purposeful withholding of action, with good intent, reaps a positive reward; and the opposite – when words which could help or heal are left unspoken, and neighbourly acts avoided – results in negative repayment. Whatever the outcome, according to the sages, what counts most is one's intention.

Speak or act with an impure mind
And trouble will follow you
As the wheel follows the ox that draws the cart

Speak or act with a pure mind
And happiness will follow you
As your shadow, unshakeable [5]

These ideas about karma are easily misunderstood. Firstly, the fruits of one's behaviour are subtle, felt at a deeply

---

5. Thomas Byrom (1976) translator, *The Dhammapada: The Sayings of the Buddha*, London: Rider Books p 21.

personal level and accumulate over time, rather than in immediate, superficial material gain or loss. Secondly, to the wise, apparent misfortune can always be turned to advantage in terms of personal development, by learning to cope with and grow through painful emotions, and so become gradually more spiritually mature in the face of adversity, of loss. On the other hand, good fortune, becoming wealthy for example, can similarly have the reverse effect, of stalling spiritual progress, such as through failing to limit a person's ability to purchase, and then get lost in, distractions from what wisdom-experts throughout the ages have uniformly described as life's major task: to grow continuously as a spiritual person.

The principle of reciprocity forms a key element in the wisdom of the so-called 'Golden Rule' that has been in circulation for centuries. One version goes like this: *'Whatever is hateful to you, do not do to your fellow'*. [6] Other versions read simply: *'Do as you would be done by'*, [7] and, *'What goes around, comes around'*.

St. Paul puts it slightly differently: *'You reap whatever you sow'*.[8] But how can people who have never prosecuted war or behaved with homicidal violence, and who are not rampant industrialists promoting unnecessary consumption, feel responsible for climate change, the misery visited upon countless refugees, and the rest?

It all makes bleak reading, but the suffering does not stop there. It gets relentlessly closer. The fullness of the situation must therefore be examined before remedies can be found and hope restored. According to the formulae of wisdom, *'Everything affects everything else'*. In the world today, multiple inter-penetrating vicious circles are operating.

Innocent people who live at a distance from places affected directly by war and disaster remain troubled. Impotent

---

6. Attributed to Hillel the Elder (born 110 BC in Babylon), a leading Jewish philosopher

7. Attributed to the Earl of Chesterfield (1694-1773)

8. Letter to the Galations, chapter 6: verse 7

onlookers, we ordinary citizens are victims too, and here is another problem. Groups that oppose the ruling forces, who use military means and other methods, are terrorists. Similarly, when groups oppose or disregard the established order for material gain, they are criminals, often involved in 'organised crime'. Both groups act consistently in their own warped interests, at the expense of the law-abiding majority. Furthermore, the two are often linked. Terrorists want weapons, for example; criminals sometimes provide them. The same kind of criminals may also be involved in preying on vulnerable refugees and migrants who become helpless fodder for financial exploitation, people smuggling, sex trafficking and worse, including murder. Yet, according to the ideals of wisdom, these are our brothers and sisters too.

All the violence and resulting devastation reciprocally fuels more division along national, political and religious fault-lines, more terrorism, political corruption, and other forms of international lawlessness such as drug production and smuggling, also money-laundering. The results threaten social breakdown, bringing more general violence and increasingly publicised, terrorist-led and crime-fuelled gun and knife attacks on civilians. Such matters, continually invading our inadequately protected lives and sensitive minds, serve to exacerbate what seems to professional eyes to be a growing epidemic of mental ill-health; for example of psychosomatic complaints, eating disorders, anxiety and depression; adding to the burden on health and social care professionals, law enforcement officers and many others in public office, forming also a perpetual drain upon the public purse.

It is all very worrying. Watching this mayhem, much of it apparently entirely senseless, leaves many feeling helpless to intervene; and so a number of strategies are employed by people to counter the sense of powerlessness and threat to self-esteem it brings on.

Possibly the commonest of these strategies involves isolating oneself, as if living behind a reinforced, transparent plastic shield, getting lost in work and home-life, in distractions of various kinds, manipulating one's environment to maximise pleasure and minimise pain; seeking the non-threatening company only of people we like, often therefore 'people-like-us', people of similar demographic profile, experiences, opinions, attitudes and values.

This is natural behaviour, normal particularly during the 'Conformist' Stage of spiritual development (See Chapter 6). Unfortunately, this method of avoiding witnessing and engaging meaningfully with the suffering of others can only have limited success: we get destructively addicted to our pleasures, or bored by them and have to seek new ones, bigger, better, faster and more thrilling, or more comforting. We also risk spending unwisely on such excesses, to the extent of running low on money and credit, some among us becoming unable or unwilling to pay for necessities like rent or food; at which point we may easily find ourselves homeless, and/or lying, cheating, stealing and harming others to accumulate the funds needed to carry on in this destructive fashion.

In this, as deep down we may be aware, we are causing injury to ourselves as much as to others, tarnishing our original, true and pristine selves. At the same time, we risk offending our most tolerant loved ones, and our less tolerant fellow lifestyle companions, perhaps finding their similar behaviour offensive in turn. As social isolation deepens, we are at risk of despising ourselves, seeing through deep into the hollowness of the immature, shallow and unwholesome ways we have adopted, unable to find a way out on our own.

In the best cases, this prompts a full re-evaluation of life and lifestyle, resulting in major changes, for example in employment, finding something more wholesome to participate in, perhaps despite having to take a pay cut. Without such a spiritual shift in perspective, however, sadly, in a state of soul-extinction, many people end their own lives. This seems unnecessary and preventable.

Unfortunately, in the prevailing culture, this is exactly

the type of pleasure-seeking, pain-avoiding lifestyle that attracts the attention of self-centred profit-seekers, keen to capitalise on the appetites for distractions and pleasures of the disadvantaged among society. This then fuels precisely the elements that contribute most to the problems in the first place: elements such as consumerist excess, through which people are encouraged at every turn to purchase objects, the latest and best, to desire and buy what we may be fooled into thinking we need and therefore must have.

The same predators seize the opportunity for gain when people desiring to escape from, or numb, the emotionally painful effects of a relentless diet of human suffering turn to using heavily promoted habit-forming drugs, whether legal or otherwise, as an alternative to feeling stressed, helpless and hopeless. The respected and sanctioned giant international pharmaceutical alcohol and tobacco companies prosper in this way, as do the more nefarious drug-dealing crime organisations with their propensity for exploiting the lives of young people and their predilection for violence. Despair is resisted and painful feelings desensitised at a cost to ordinary people that is often under-estimated. Furthermore, the use and abuse of habit-forming medications and other intoxicating substances are often combined with other destructive, difficult and costly to treat addictions.

Damaged self-esteem, helplessness and worthlessness are often accompanied by feelings of both hopelessness and emptiness, a profound hollowness of the soul, that cannot be filled except, in the final analysis, by spiritual energy, by compassion and love. This does not prevent people in ignorance, however, trying quite desperately to fill their near-bottomless, inner void with anything that seems to provide at least temporary relief. At the literal level, for example, the most obvious way to fill yourself is by eating. The phrase 'comfort eating' attests to this; and the growing epidemic in affluent populations of overeating, and its direct corollary, obesity, offers evidence supporting this interpretation. The modern scourge of anorexia nervosa, as a likely direct over-reaction against this trend, provides further evidence.

Additional common activities risking addiction include obsessive shopping, social media fixation, gaming, gambling, pornography and compulsive sexual behaviour. These further fuel consumerism and it is worth noting to what extent they are all promoted via the internet, giving access without supervision or effective external control, adding to the tendency for people to remain detrimentally fixed in social isolation. Online gambling is widely accepted and advertised. Pornography is freely available, even to children and young adolescents. Considerable restraint is therefore required to manage one's online activities, suggesting individual self-discipline as another key aspect of wisdom, a challenge to acquire at first, perhaps, but easier to come by eventually, and ultimately liberating, because it develops naturally alongside spiritual maturity.

Drug-taking, gambling and pornography are also likely to be linked to organised crime and money-laundering enterprises, so the circles go round and round. Currently, consumer culture not only tolerates but, through only limited sanctions, can be said to actively promote this situation, in ways that are clearly harmful for individual psychological well-being and overall social health. Cannabis, a relatively safe drug, is already legal for so-called 'recreational' use in some parts of the world. Not everyone would say this was wise. There are better ways of achieving inner calm and joyfulness without either risking serious mental health problems, or spending money to fund either legal profiteers or less scrupulous criminal providers.

* * *

On reflection, then, what emerges is the overview of a great, malign, destructive process, forever turning the circles, deadening souls, and tightening the screws of human suffering. Feeling helpless in the face of it, people quite reasonably ask the question, 'What else can we do?' For some, becoming an activist is the answer, joining with others, writing letters, signing petitions of protest, and going on marches. When this is entirely peaceful and without rancour, it is to be applauded, whether effective in producing the desired change or not, because it brings people out of isolation, coming together in harmony to reflect their mutual, mature and healthy concerns. Also praiseworthy is the determination of many to alter their lifestyles according to the needs of the times, aiming at reduction in fossil fuel usage, for example, embracing waste-recycling, dietary change away from meat consumption and so on. But this book is less about doing than about being and becoming, about working towards growth and maturity. Born of wisdom, timely and effective actions can be relied upon to follow when the way forward becomes clear.

Wisdom is the best remedy for all the complex inter-related ills of humankind outlined above. It is the most reliable antidote to the folly and greed that has brought about the predicament we all face, that our children must address, and their children, their grand-children and all future generations will inherit if the causes are allowed to persist.

The solution to these problems is simply stated. It involves many people improving their sense of connection – on an individual, person by person, basis – to the sacred unity of creation, allowing its healing influence to dwell within, enabling them to grow, however gradually, in terms of spiritual awareness, surrendering to the healthiest of impulses to join freely with others in caring and kinship, in kindness, compassion and love. That is what wisdom is about. That is why, without delay, each in our own way, we would do well to think deeply about, go seek, and start gaining in wisdom.

What we have to be is what we are.

* * *

2

WISDOM, SPIRITUAL EXPERIENCE, AND LOVE

The findings of science provide good evidence that all people are connected to one another, and equally to everything else in the universe. To begin with, *physics and chemistry* teach us that everything originated billions of years ago with the 'Big Bang'; that the first stars, formed of hydrogen and helium gases, eventually burned away and finally blew apart with such tremendous force as to create and spread wide all the atoms of the periodic table, leading to the creation of a multitude of galaxies, including our own, our solar system and planets.

The same stardust atoms, *biology* says, contribute to carbon-based life-forms that share a genetic heritage and evolutionary pathway towards the astonishing diversity and sophistication of life on earth today. Animals require an atmosphere containing oxygen, a gas in the air that we humans all breathe and share, which is produced in green plants by photosynthesis, a process that depends on entrapping light energy from the sun, our local star. We humans, like other animals, make use of oxygen then exhale it combined with carbon (as carbon dioxide), whereupon it is taken back up by plants and re-used in a continuous cycle. It is clear from observations like this that we are each inextricably bound up with nature.

P*sychology* reveals, in addition, that human beings share universal faculties, among them the five senses: being able to learn, think, calculate and reason; the impulses and ability to speak and act; also a range of emotions, both painful and pleasurable. *Sociology and anthropology* have in turn revealed significant commonalities of social groupings and behaviour.

These findings allow us at least an intellectual grasp of cosmic inter-connections. We can also develop significantly further this understanding of universal unity through the exercise of our imagination; but to know it personally, as a deeply seated, life-changing, indelible and incontrovertible truth depends on something else. Some would say it requires the direct perceptive capacity of a human soul. It is, in other words, a matter of spiritual experience.

* * *

The paradox involved, whereby spiritual experiences are easy to ignore, is best explained by an analogy. Consider what it might be like to ride in a hot air balloon: the wind blows you along, but because your vehicle keeps exact pace with the draught, you do not feel it on your skin. Similarly, the great spiritual breath or holy wind of the universe constantly propels and steers us along, but we may only become aware of it when, for example, it seems significantly to alter pace, change direction or fall away. As a result, many people claim no personal knowledge of the spiritual dimension of their lives. Those who do, describe a number of different types of experience. One of these in particular reflects the sense of cosmic unity already mentioned:

Awareness that all things are one.

A good example is given by research psychologist, Steve Taylor, who records twenty-year-old Emma describing how, during a lengthy episode of depression, she picked up a marble and started playing with it, whereupon the familiar world melted away, a vision of beauty and perfection suddenly in its place. She told Dr Taylor:

> *I saw reality as simply this perfect one-ness... Everything felt just right. The marble seemed a reflection of the universe. All my 'problems' and suffering seemed meaningless, ridiculous... There was a feeling of acceptance and oneness. It was a moment of enlightenment.*[9]

This description gives us an example of 'holism', where a small part of a larger whole accurately symbolises and reflects that greater unity. In this case the holistic revelation was powerful enough to release Emma from her depression.

* * *

In the year 2000, five per cent of a large British sample described having this particular type of thing happen in their lives. In addition, over three-quarters (76%) admitted having some kind of spiritual experience. The people surveyed were responding to the following question:

> *Have you ever been aware of or influenced by a presence or a power, whether you call it God or not, that is different from your everyday self?*

This question was originally posed by Oxford zoologist, Alister Hardy, who set up the 'Religious Experience Research Centre' [10] in 1969; and the Centre now houses an archive of over 6,000 accounts of first-hand spiritual or

---

9. Steve Taylor (2011) *Out of the Darkness: From turmoil to transformation.* London: Hay House, p.8.

10. See Appendix 2 for website details.

religious experiences of people from across the world. In 1987, researchers David Hay and Gordon Heald looked at the collection carefully. Selecting the most common experiences, they defined eight subcategories as follows:

1. Awareness that all things are one
2. Awareness of a patterning of events (synchronicity)
3. Awareness of the presence of God
4. Awareness of a presence not named
5. Awareness of prayers being answered
6. Awareness of a sacred presence in nature
7. Awareness of the presence of the dead
8. Awareness of an evil presence.

Questions about six of these were included in the BBC's 2000 *'Soul of Britain'* review of the spiritual state of the nation, the largest ever survey of the personal beliefs and attitudes of the people of Britain.

* * *

Awareness of a patterning of events (synchronicity)

According to the BBC survey, this is the most frequently occurring type of experience, described by over half the sample (55%). Author Michael Shearer says the same: *'Synchronicity, meaningful coincidence, is not a weird rarity, it is common and frequent'.*[11]

This experience often encourages people to speak in terms of 'fate', 'destiny', 'karma', 'kismet', 'Providence', and also 'God's will'. To give a personal example, one day in England a family friend, knowing I was about to travel to Australia, wrote down the name of his close friend from Melbourne, telling me that if I looked him up I would be assured of a fine

---

11. Michael Shearer (2014) *Walking a Rainbow*, CreateSpace, Amazon, p10.

welcome. I did not go to Melbourne, but some months later I did become friendly with a woman in Sydney who told me about her brother who was resident there. Imagine her surprise when I showed her the piece of paper from my wallet with her brother's name and details on it. I am a matter-of-fact kind of person but, where wisdom is concerned, it pays to take account of the extraordinary, and this was one of a number of synchronicities which happened to me at that time, providing cosmic-style reassurance that I was on track, in the right place, and doing the right thing.

How often do we hear people, whether they acknowledge a spiritual dimension or not, say of something that, *'It was meant to be'*, or, perhaps consoling others, *'It was just not meant to be'*? This may not simply be an example of so-called 'superstition' at odds with the findings of science and therefore to be dismissed. Shearer has admitted that synchronicity is not yet a scientifically documented phenomenon. *'But if it happens'*, he continues later in his book, *'Then physics is somehow radically misconceived. If things can happen which are not just effects of physical causes, but have meaning for those who experience them, and happen because of the meaning, then the world works in a way which includes meaning and metaphor. The world is a poetic place.'* [12] We will look at this again after going through the remainder of the list.

* * *

Awareness of the presence of God,
and
Awareness of a presence not named

Because they are broadly similar, only the first was used in the BBC study. The word 'God' can, of course, be contentious,

---

12. Ibid., p 36.

particularly because people feel called upon either to 'believe' or 'disbelieve' in God, or to admit that they are undecided. This kind of experience is helpful when it occurs in someone's life, because it goes beyond that potentially divisive situation. Two people can have a similar experience, but use different language to describe it.

The *'Twelve-Step Programmes'* for addiction, for example, introduced in America in 1939 by Alcoholics Anonymous and copied later throughout the world for use with other addictions, importantly introduces a spiritual component to the recovery programme. Steps 2 and 3, for example, read:

> *We came to believe that a power greater than ourselves could restore us to sanity* [and so]... *made a decision to turn our will and our lives over to the care of God* as we understood Him'.[13]

One commentator, Herbert Spencer, has added:

> *'Most of us think this awareness of a power greater than ourselves is the essence of spiritual experience. Our more religious members [of AA] call it 'God-consciousness'.'*[14]

When I had been in Australia almost six years, something like this occurred to me. After deciding to return, soon before my departure for Britain, I woke early one morning and went into the hillside garden where I was staying. I recall the wonderful views across the city towards the ocean from that beautiful vantage point. Sitting on the grass by the swimming pool, alert to the warmth of the sun, the mottled colours of the eucalyptus trees and the lyrical sound of birdsong, I fell into a kind of reverie during which I felt incredibly safe, in the

---

13. Alcoholics Anonymous (2001) p 59.

14. Ibid., Appendix II, p 568.

presence of some divine protective force or energy, as if being lovingly cradled. I had been apprehensive at the prospect of returning to my home country without much of a plan, but in that peaceful moment felt entirely assured that everything would be made clear in due course, and would work out fine... As it did!

* * *

Awareness of prayers being answered

When David Hay wrote about the BBC survey,[15] he gave a number of examples of this, including that of a man who had been treated for three years for a serious and debilitating form of mental illness who reported that, when he had reached utter despair, he wept and prayed to God for mercy. That cold, starry night, standing in the grounds of the psychiatric hospital, waiting with other patients to be let back into the ward, he experienced someone standing beside him and a voice saying, *'Mad or sane, you are one of my sheep'*. It gave him strength and courage. When, twenty years later, he spoke of it for the first time, he said the experience was entirely positive, calling it, *'The pivot of my life'*.

* * *

Awareness of a sacred presence in nature

Michael Shearer's book tells of the 500-mile pilgrimage to Santiago de Compostela that he made some years ago with his 9-year-old son, Kes. Appearing to have had a number of spiritual experiences along the way, here he is describing what occurred on a steep path in the Spanish mountains:

---

15. David Hay (2006) *Something there: The Biology of the Human Spirit*. Darton, Longman and Todd pp17-18

We were above it all, liberated into a massive space. It was exhilarating... We walked in a state of exuberance. It was heady and magical. I felt like singing. Energy gushed up through me like a spiritual oil well. It was special here... The sense of euphoria grew and grew. It took over until I was just one glorious bubble of bliss... My self had opened and opened & in had flowed the energy of the mountains & the sky. I was ecstatic. [16]

* * *

Awareness of the presence of the dead

As an example, David Hay writes of a mother who heard from her son's school that he had been taken ill with polio. In her words:

As I lay across the kitchen table in complete anguish and despair, I distinctly felt my grandmother's hand laid on my shoulder and I had the feeling of complete serenity.

Her grandmother had died years earlier. Her son survived the life-threatening infection unharmed, as the woman had immediately felt sure he would, following the comforting visitation from her relative.[17]

Many ghost-like situations have been recorded of people appearing to others at around the time of their death. An example recorded by David Lorimer involved a woman reading at home, *'When she suddenly had a vision of her aunt in the doorway.'* She checked her watch and it was 4.45

16. Michael Shearer (2014) *Walking a Rainbow*, CreateSpace, Amazon pp 250-1

17. David Hay (2006) *Something There: The Biology of the Human Spirit,* London: Darton, Longman and Todd Ltd. p 21.

pm. Later she discovered that the aunt had died elsewhere at exactly the same time as the vision had appeared.[18]

Such experiences are often reported during the immediate period of grief after a loved one has died, and are frequently found to be comforting.

* * *

The final type of spiritual experience, in contrast, is often more alarming than the others:

Awareness of an evil presence.

One of David Hay's examples came from a woman travelling by car in a foreign country, then finding a place to stay in a large town.

> *On entering the room I felt a most terrible chill, a fear I had never known. I am afraid I cannot put into words what exactly I felt, only to say that some terrible presence was in the room also.[19]*

One aspect of spiritual experiences this account demonstrates is their 'ineffability', meaning that they are beyond description in everyday language, which is one of the reasons why people tend to stay quiet about them. Further reasons given by David Hay after interviewing a different set of people, chosen because *'they never went to church'*, concerned being afraid of two things: being laughed at, or being preached at. When certain that neither was happening, Hay reports, they opened up and spoke freely. All could definitely identify spiritual aspects to their lives. None later

---

18. David Lorimer (2017) *Survival? Death as a Transition*. Hove: White Crow Books pp 209-10.

19. Hay (2006), p 21.

had any regrets about speaking up, and most felt they had profited from the opportunity to reflect on and talk about these deeply personal matters.

To have an experience involving awareness of an evil presence often seems to prove disturbing, accompanied by feelings of misery or dread, but not always. One woman is mentioned by Hay who, after seeing photographs of dead and emaciated corpses piled high, the murdered victims of Nazi concentration camps, when thirteen years old, described some 'dark insistence' that took her over for hours, 'as if pummelling her brain'. As the unpleasant experience dissipated, she was left with the confident and promising idea that she should become a doctor, which she later did without any subsequent regrets.[20]

* * *

Returning to Michael Shearer's comments that, if synchronicity is a real and reliable phenomenon; if indeed, *'the world works in a way which includes meaning and metaphor'*, and, *'physics is somehow radically misconceived';* there is a strong argument in favour of a new, expanded paradigm for science.

A shift is needed to include a theory of human consciousness (of understanding, interpretation and the attribution of meaning) that has effects cutting across time and space. Consciousness is necessarily involved right down to the molecular and atomic levels of material existence, which implies some kind of integral and deeply personal association with a transcendent universal force or energy, breath or wind; thus a seamless connection between individual people and a 'holy spirit'. That many leading scientists and researchers are also now calling for such a paradigm shift can be seen in the publications of the Scientific and Medical Network,[21] and books like Steve

---

20. Ibid., p 22.

21. See Appendix 2 for website details.

Taylor's *'Spiritual Science'*[22] and Tom McLeish's *'The Poetry and Music of Science'*. [23] It is also the main argument behind, and purpose of, the extremely well-backed and influential Galileo Commission.[24]

A similar theory would be useful to account as well for so-called 'paranormal' experiences; including telepathy, perception at a distance (extra-sensory perception [ESP] or 'clairvoyance'), perception through time, mind-matter interaction, and mental interaction with living organisms.[25] Whether these can also be said to amount to spiritual experiences remains uncertain, but they appear to lie on a similar spectrum.

It is important to add that this is by no means a complete catalogue of possibilities, that there are different and more subtle forms of spiritual experience also available, depending on the keenness of one's spiritual eyesight. By way of explanation, we can once again use the example of balloon flight. Although we cannot feel the spiritual wind on our faces, we can notice its effect elsewhere as we travel over the ground below, and similarly as we observe people as they move along in other balloons close by. Looking carefully, we might see, for example, the beautiful ripple and swirling effect of air movement on the tall wheat growing in the fields, and the crested wavelets created by wind on the lake beneath us. We may observe other balloons changing direction, speeding up or slowing down before ours does. There are many things to watch out for, giving an indication of a spiritual dimension affecting our lives; the radiant smile of a small child, for

---

22. Steve Taylor (2018) *Spiritual Science: why science needs spirituality to make sense of the world*. London: Watkins.

23. Tom McLeish (2019) *The Poetry and Music of Science*. Oxford: Oxford University Press.

24. See Appendix 2 for website details.

25. The list is taken from Dean Radin (1997) *The Conscious Universe: the scientific truth of psychic phenomena*. San Francisco: Harper Edge.

example, sunlight glinting off early morning dew, or the intoxicating fragrance of a rose. As Thomas Merton once wrote: *'The gate of heaven is everywhere'*. [26] All we need to do sometimes is to slow down, avoid distraction, and pay closer attention.

* * *

Reliable methods for enhancing one's capacity for honing spiritual skills and our capacity for this kind of awareness will be discussed later, notably in Chapters 15 and 16. Beforehand, special mention is worthy here of the concept of love which, like beauty, has a markedly spiritual quality.

At its most wholesome, mature love does not depend on any 'ifs'. It is unconditional, neither possessive, nor erotic. This, the purest form of love, is entirely imbued with a sense of seamless and utter connection with the loved-one, the loved object or activity. When someone says, *'I love my work'*, for example, *'I love my garden'*, *'I love playing* (a particular) *sport'*, or perhaps, *'I love reading'*, this implies non-separateness, the timeless experience of getting lost in the activity, being 'in the zone'. One's personal ego-sensation is in abeyance, subordinated fully to engagement with the matter in hand. We find ourselves operating with skill, intuition, creativity and flexibility, performing at peak level, extracting meaning from our activity, a sense of purpose and self-worth; often, too, a feeling of belonging. It is in this relinquishing of ego and adoption of selflessness that wisdom, love and spirituality go together.

Human relations are complex, ranging from being cool, distant and diffident, on one hand, to being 'enmeshed', over-involved, fractious and highly emotionally charged on the other. Loving relations, at their healthiest and most

---

26. Thomas Merton (1966) *Conjectures of a Guilty Bystander,* New York: Doubleday & Company, Inc. p 142.

wholesome, though, similarly imply non-separateness, warmth and affection, of belonging to the other in ways that seems both eternal and 'meant to be'. These are spiritual qualities and when such love is achieved and experienced between two people (who may be partners throughout life), they are in effect 'soul-mates', a situation reflecting spiritual friendship that strongly suggests itself as the ideal model for interactions and inter-relationships between all people, based on kinship and kindness.

Such a conclusion follows what spiritual teachers throughout the ages have said, one way or another: that the universe itself is the supreme embodiment of love energy. When we feel love, we are connecting with the great sacred whole of creation and likewise, when we feel deeply connected to the whole, to all others and to nature, we will experience love. The experience of feeling loved helps us along the spiritual path, in particular because it helps us each discover and develop our capacity for self-love. This is very different from selfishness, from the self-centred, self-important attitudes and behaviour of personal immaturity that owes more to self-doubt than true self-confidence. Bearing in mind , for example, that Jesus of Nazareth called upon people to *'Love your neighbour as yourself'*,[27] being capable of loving oneself unconditionally becomes important.

Sometimes a person is fortunate enough to experience a breakthrough recognition of universal love, both in the world and in his or her own life. Here is an example. Thomas Merton was a monk who lived from the age of 26 in a monastery in rural Kentucky.[28] He wrote a famous book,[29] and became well-known throughout America and elsewhere; but by 1958, when he was 43, it is clear from his diary entries that he was

---

27. The Gospel According to Luke, chapter 10: verse 27.

28. The Abbey of Our Lady of Gethsemani, Trappist, Ky. See: www.merton.org.

29. Thomas Merton (1948) *The Seven Storey Mountain*. New York: Harcourt, Brace & Company.

worried about being cut off from people in the world outside the cloister. On 18th March that year, Merton was in the town of Louisville going to a printer on monastery business when he had a revelation, describing it like this:

At the corner of Fourth and Walnut, in the center of the shopping district, I was suddenly overwhelmed with the realization that I loved all those people, that they were mine and I theirs, that we could not be alien to one another even though we were total strangers. It was like waking from a dream of separateness... [30]

It was as if Merton, travelling alone in his own balloon, suddenly looked up and noticed all the other people in their balloons being blown along by the same cosmic breath or holy spirit, and that they were thereby permanently joined together in harmony and love.

Merton was immediately grateful. *Thank God that I am like other(s)'*, he wrote, going on to explain that at each person's centre is:

A point of nothingness... A point of pure truth... The pure glory of God in us... It is like a pure diamond, blazing with the invisible light of heaven. It is in everybody, and if we could see it, we would see these billions of points of light coming together in the face and blaze of a sun that would make all the darkness and cruelty of life vanish completely.[31]

Merton's gift was being able to put his experience poetically into words, using metaphor and imaginative representation, for what was otherwise inexpressible. Note, too, his inclusion of paradox: *'A point of nothingness'* and *'invisible light'* do

30. Thomas Merton (1966) *Conjectures of a Guilty Bystander,* pp 140-1. Walnut Street has since been renamed Mohammed Ali Boulevard.

31. Ibid., pp 141-2.

not make ordinary sense; but there is no other way to conjure up an image of divinity. His use of the word 'God' reflects his Christian faith (although it is a fact that Merton was highly knowledgeable about and sympathetic to the truths to be found in all major world faith traditions). Others may prefer different language to indicate a holy spirit, a divine and unifying source of cosmic energy flowing constantly throughout the unfolding universe.

Few among us are likely to be as spiritually gifted as Merton, but his vision gives us all hope as we grow in maturity, finding ways to improve our awareness of the spiritual realm and the sacred breath within each of us that gives us life, love, wisdom, drive, direction, purpose and meaning. All we must do to maintain progress is keep ourselves topped up with the spiritual love energy of the universe by finding ways of connecting with it regularly, frequently, and for as long as we can.

One way to begin, or take the search further, would be to think more often and more deeply about our private aims, ambitions and priorities, to think about our most heartfelt values. Think, for example, about how you interact with other people, how you fit in with the world of nature, and with the greater whole of existence. What gives your life meaning? From what, and who, do you derive direction, courage, inner strength, hope and a sense of purpose? What makes you feel alive?

This entire book is designed to help readers focus on important life questions like these. The ideas presented so far, and in the following chapters, should not either be taken as true or rejected outright as false. They are for taking reasonably seriously, for playing around with (but purposefully). The essential task involved is one of contemplation; the call being as much to mature reflection and discussion, as it may be to action.

To go along with this, then, will involve finding others to discuss such matters with; people to listen to, learn from, and doubtless also to teach. It means making soul-friends, joining fellow pilgrims on life's spiritual path, people who recognise each other for their shared wisdom and values, for their kindness and compassion towards one another, even (perhaps especially) towards those who ignore, undermine, criticise and attack them. This would be to promote and re-invigorate what might be called a 'world wide Wave of Wisdom',[32] correcting the trajectory of human development and evolution that seems to have gone awry, starting with Descartes and his followers (see Author's Notes, page 161). Nothing that might help the flow of humankind back in the direction of what is most healthy and wholesome could be too little, and it is never too late.

* * *

---

32. See Appendix 2 for website details.

3

MORE FUEL FOR REFLECTION: FOUR RELATED SETS OF IDEAS

It may seem illogical, opposing the notion that spiritual experience is important for the gaining of wisdom, but there are ways to grow wiser using one's intellect; through thinking things through. This and the remaining chapters in Part One therefore cover four sets of related ideas as fuel for such consideration.

* * *

The first set has already been described briefly; that wisdom is served best by considering the human predicament according to five seamlessly inter-linked dimensions of human understanding and experience. These are:

Physical (energy and matter) – the miracle of existence;
Biological (organs and organisms) – the miracle of life;
Psychological (mental activity) – the miracle of consciousness;
Social (relationships) – the miracle of love; and
Spiritual (souls and the sacred) – the miracle of unity.

Everything concerning human beings – health and sickness, for example – can be seen to operate through all five dimensions. The spiritual dimension, taking pride of place, appears to people as embodying an originating principle, seamlessly creating, linking and shaping the other four.

Science seeks factual knowledge through being 'objective', reducing the effects of unreliable human intervention. Reference to *'dimensions of human understanding and experience'*, on the other hand, emphasises the value of knowledge and experiences that are personal and, in contrast, 'subjective'. This helpfully restores the individual to the centre of consideration. Dogmatic statements of so-called 'objective' proof are thus avoided. A question like, 'Does God exist?' is unanswerable from this evidence-seeking perspective. Less divisive and more relevant is a question such as, 'Have you, or anyone you know and trust, ever experienced something that seemed like a miracle?' or, 'Have you ever found yourself totally lost in awe and wonder at some aspect of the mysterious workings of nature and the universe?' or, again, 'Have you ever felt yourself in the presence of, or affected by, some kind of divine power or being?'

* * *

A second set of related ideas involves considering life as a journey towards wisdom and maturity, where both good or pleasurable and bad or painful experiences can help people learn and develop through six recognizable stages:

1. *Egocentric* (immature, self-referenced existence)
2. *Conditioning* (learning by absorption from strong family and social traditions)
3. *Conformist* (seeking to belong, mainly by choosing to follow social trends and conventions)
4. *Individual* (starting to think, speak and act independently)

5. *Integration* (shifting values and behaviour towards altruism, through recognising one's deep kinship with fellow human beings, with nature and everything else)
6. *Universal* (achieving maturity and wisdom, becoming a natural teacher and compassionate healer)

Everyone's growth develops along such a pathway. At any moment, some will have gone further than others, but it is unwise to think of it competitively, or in terms of some people being superior or inferior to others. It is better to hold one's focus upon one's own spiritual journey and its requirements for progress. There are different tasks, attitudes and priorities at each stage.

In Stage 1 (in infancy), these are concerned with safety, survival and comfort, seeking to fulfil natural likes and dislikes, having little distinction between spiritual and everyday awareness.

In Stage 2 (during childhood), they involve learning (about the world in general, and especially about traditions, rules and conventions) with diminishing attention to spiritual awareness as time passes, during which the secular, scientific, materialist worldview becomes dominant.

In Stage 3, strong attachments and aversions are made and consolidated, reflecting a natural desire to further one's interest in personal gratification and social integration. This is achieved through acquisition of prized allegiances, status and possessions, and the denial or rejection of whatever seems uncomfortable, alien and contradictory.

In Stage 4, priorities involve discovering and developing oneself as an independent and responsible observer, as well as participant, in one's own life, relinquishing former attachments and adjusting to the resulting uncertainty and relative isolation.

In Stage 5, the emphasis shifts towards re-evaluation of one's values and behaviour from a universal perspective, bringing one's life increasingly into line with the highest altruistic ideals.

In Stage 6, life's intrinsic meaning is revealed, understood and accepted fully. Being, rather than doing or achieving, is given priority, with the result of living in the moment, without fear of further loss, or even of death.

The first two stages are discussed further in Chapter 11, on 'Education' and the last two are addressed in greater detail in Chapter 15, 'Towards Maturity'. Here the discussion begins with Stages 3 and 4 because, according to research, the majority of people past their teens have reached one or other of these, or lie between the two. In general society today, then, 'This is where we are'. Culturally, we remain adolescent.

In explaining these middle stages, it is necessary to emphasise that each person is subject to, and therefore may struggle with, two contrasting drives:

i) To conform within family and society, and,
ii) To think, speak and act independently.

In Stage 3, we tend to adhere, whether rigidly or flexibly, to the culture, authority, values, belief systems (including religious/secular and political belief systems), laws, customs, allegiances (for example, to nation or sports team), rituals and other behavioural practices of the family, communal group and society at large. There is comfort and safety in belonging, with the risk of being ostracised and ridiculed, of feeling threatened and possibly being preached at, when showing signs of being different.

Nevertheless, as horizons broaden, contact and familiarity with different people, cultures, conventions, belief systems and so on, tend to result in review and revision of previous allegiances. Pressure grows to re-think priorities and take increasing responsibility for thoughts, feelings and intentions; also for one's words and actions; equally and importantly, for what one does not say and avoids doing. This is to enter Stage 4, a key step towards personal maturity; but there is still some distance to travel.

* * *

A third set of ideas relates to the notion that progress on this journey towards personal maturity occurs most commonly through the transformational effects of suffering. The psychological processes associated with loss, pain, healing and growth will therefore be described in the next chapter. It follows that, in principle, it is better to face and accept suffering, to make it meaningful and profit from it, rather than seek to avoid it.

This challenges the prevailing attitude within western culture, whereby both physical and emotional pain are widely considered regrettable, to be eradicated or suppressed. Rather than take responsibility for their own suffering, people are quick to blame other people, governments, giant corporations, religious institutions, or other organisations, for not doing enough to prevent or remove pain. The emotional healing process is as natural and reliable, under advantageous conditions, as the healing of cuts, abrasions and fractures. It is easier to assume responsibility when this is explained and understood and when a hopeful outcome is assured.

Being trained and lovingly encouraged in matters of self-discipline when young prepares a person for taking personal responsibility later. This is important because the collective progress of humanity towards wisdom depends on increasing numbers of people taking responsibility on an individual by individual basis, generation by generation, until what might be called a 'worldwide wave of wisdom' swells to its maximum and a universal tipping-point of spiritual maturity is reached.

Underpinning this is the spiritual concept of reciprocity, according to which thoughts, words and actions intending either good or harm, whether towards another person, group or the environment in which people live, rebound in some way on oneself, for better or worse.

When a person wishes for, intends or does good, acting kindly and thoughtfully, they will benefit. In contrast, when a person wishes for, intends or actually brings about harm, acting destructively through deliberate mischief or cruelty, or through careless neglect, they will eventually in consequence suffer, but not necessarily in worldly terms. Often insensitive to it, they suffer in the spiritual dimension through diminished contact with the unified cosmic whole, the holy breath or spirit, the sacred unity that forms the greatest source of energy, direction, sustenance, courage and hope; through impoverishment, in other words, of the soul.

People suffer, however, only until they learn and mature. Wisdom recognises the principle of reciprocity not as a punitive mechanism, but as one providing balance and guidance. Apparent misfortune involving loss frequently offers an opportunity for growth.

* * *

A fourth set of ideas forming a thread throughout this book concerns two complementary ways of thinking, of experiencing and interacting with the world. These will be discussed in more detail in Chapter 5, '*One Brain – Two Ways of Thinking*'; however it seems sensible to introduce the distinction between 'binary' and 'unitary' mental activity here.

The binary or 'dualist' approach involves *either/or, black/white, right/wrong, us/them, win/lose, success/failure* type thinking, and is easily, therefore, divisive. The unitary or 'holistic' approach, on the other hand, involves inclusive *both/and* type thinking. It is, therefore, unifying. Materialistic and worldly, dualism is at the centre of human scientific and technical endeavour. The unitary approach, in contrast, informing wisdom and compassion, lies at the heart of human spirituality, seeing people as equals, regardless of gender, sexuality, skin colour, age, race, creed or anything else.

Dualism and holism are both useful and complement each other, but in secular western culture the binary approach has become dominant, resulting in many problems and much human suffering. Personal (and ultimately collective) wisdom and maturity depend on a corrective re-balancing where these patterns of thought are concerned. This, too, affects the values adopted by individuals and society, as discussed further in Chapter 7.

* * *

4

THREAT, LOSS, PAIN, HEALING, AND GROWTH

Emotions are vital to a sense of being alive, contributing significantly to a person's sense of meaning and purpose. They are valuable indicators of spiritual experience as when people are, for example, 'filled with awe and wonder', 'racked with tears and grief', 'paralysed with fear', 'overwhelmed by a sense of peace and tranquillity', or 'ecstatic with joy'. In the development of wisdom, emotional sensitivity and self-awareness are at least as important as cognitive intelligence, especially as human emotions operate more logically than is often realised.

Table 1 offers the idea of a spectrum of eight complementary pairs of painful and pain-free cognitive-emotions.[33] According to this scheme, for example, happiness is paired with its polar opposite, sadness. When one is present, the other is, by definition, absent. This does not mean that they cannot alternate, often rapidly, and so appear to mingle. It is the same with regard to the other pairs, clarity with bewilderment, for

---

33. They are called 'cognitive emotions' because cognition (thinking) is required to give each emotional sensation its name.

example. The reason for identifying these pairs will become clear in due course.

Table 1[34]
The spectrum of eight complementary cognitive-emotional pairs

<u>Painful</u>	<u>Pain-free</u>
Wanting (desire/aversion)	Contentment (satisfaction)
Bewilderment	Clarity
Anxiety	Calm
Doubt	Certainty
Anger	Acquiescence (Acceptance)
Shame	Worth
Guilt	Innocence (Purity)
Sadness	Happiness (Joy)

Emotions are invested in many things: in people, for example, in places, possessions, activities, in ideas and ideologies. This is 'attachment'. Furthermore, *wanting* to win, for instance, is naturally accompanied by *not wanting* to lose, thus each attachment is accompanied by a correspondingly opposed 'aversion'. Attachments and aversions provide the conditions for emotional pain through reversals of fortune. Not having what you desire yields a measure of suffering.

34. Adapted from Larry Culliford (2011) *The Psychology of Spirituality: An Introduction*, London: Jessica Kingsley Publishers p 22.

Equally, securing one's object of attachment immediately sets up the condition of *threat*, the threat of harm, damage or *loss*.

The whole spectrum of feelings is involved. To put it briefly, threats provoke and promote the painful emotions of *bewilderment, anxiety* and *doubt*. Attacks (on one's person, possessions, opinions or beliefs, for example) threatening loss, may provoke *anger*. Impending loss engenders feelings of *shame* and *guilt* (through feeling responsible). Actual losses give rise finally to *sadness*, allowing the cycle of emotional pain to diminish and eventually fade away.

This works, because sadness is the key to healthy grieving. It involves 'letting go', the freeing up and relinquishing of attachments. The cleansing ('catharsis'), of tears and the other accompaniments of grief, permit the loosening ('lysis') of emotional investment in the object of loss, commencing the miracle of healing. As painful feelings die down, each is transformed into its pain-free complementary opposite. Bewilderment, anxiety and doubt shift towards *clarity, calm* and *certainty*. Anger softens into *acceptance*. Shame and guilt give way to *purity, self-worth* and *innocence*. Sadness is transformed into *joy*.

Calm, joy and acceptance are the emotions of wisdom, characterised by greater equanimity and resilience than is usual during the earlier stages of personal development, when it is entirely natural for people to resist change. Even the threat of change can arouse anger, which is often accompanied by a strong sense of being 'in the right'. This is a destructive, and ultimately self-destructive, trap to avoid. Those who feel right, but are in fact mistaken about something, would do well to pause before acting on their emotions. Those who are correct also would do well to remain patient in the face of threats and challenges while their anger subsides, remaining confident that their point of view will be upheld by events as they unfold, knowing too that a calmer frame of mind will be more persuasive than an aggressive one.

Just as certain conditions must be met for cuts and

abrasions to heal, so it is with emotional pain and trauma. Skin is weak and heals poorly in people who are undernourished, lacking essential proteins and vitamins. Wounds do not heal if they are too big, dirty, or become infected. Doctors and nurses do not heal the damage, but they do try to ensure the proper conditions, through administering antiseptics and antibiotic medication, for example, also by applying sutures and bandaging.

Emotional healing similarly proceeds best when certain advantageous conditions are met. It goes more smoothly when the affected person feels safe from further psychological threats and losses. Protection comes from feeling secure, valued and loved, from living in an environment of affection, trust and hope for the future, and depends therefore on healthy family relationships, and similarly on prevailing, conflict-free community and cultural interactions. Here, then, we discover another helpful pointer towards wisdom.

And there is more. Emotional healing carries a valuable bonus. Personal growth is a direct and reliable natural consequence. After successfully surviving a loss, people become less fearful of what might happen in the future, less regretful of what has happened in the past, and less anxious generally. They become more spontaneous, better able to live 'in the moment', better equipped to engage anew with people and places, with fresh activities; and better able, too, to sit still and quietly appreciate beauty, to contemplate life's path and ponder its values. This is how experiencing and enduring suffering through to the culmination of the healing process contributes towards spiritual maturity.

Moving forward, people will still experience attachments, desires and aversions, and so be susceptible to painful emotions like those listed. Nevertheless, experiencing and enduring adversity helps individuals to develop increasing emotional resilience and stability. They grow wiser, calmer, happier, clearer in mind and more confident. They become less inward-looking, angry, guilty and ashamed. In addition, although less frequently sorrowful, they nevertheless come to value sadness when it arises as a sign of growth, for example when feeling sad in sympathy with the misfortunes of others. The other side of this, well worth mentioning, is 'sympathetic joy', according to which we also feel delight in the good fortune of others.

People who have endured losses tend naturally to become more outward-looking, thus increasingly aware of the plight and suffering of their fellow human beings similarly susceptible to attachments, losses, accidents, injuries, mental afflictions, ill-health, ageing, and, finally, death. The awakening to this new awareness, that everyone suffers, brings vital energy to people's natural tendencies towards empathy and compassion, the insight ensuring that people become increasingly neighbourly, more useful and valuable to others in their suffering.

Knowing that, ultimately, all pain may be shared, makes a person wise, better able to face life's many challenges, twists and turns, its ups and downs, including perhaps the most definitive challenge of dying. Everyone eventually loses all worldly possessions and human connections, being finally called on to relinquish all attachments and aversions as their body ceases to function. Growing in maturity through suffering is good preparation for that inevitable eventuality. It is a sure sign of maturity when a person can experience emotional suffering – their own and that of other people – without turning away. Another clear indication is the readiness to face death with a smile.

* * *

5

ONE BRAIN – TWO
WAYS OF THINKING

The two distinctive 'binary' and 'unitary' types of thinking mentioned in Chapter 3 depend on the human brain having two hemispheres. With more than 100 billion densely interconnected nerve cells, according to psychiatrist, neuroscience expert and accomplished author, Iain McGilchrist, *'There may be more connections in the human brain than particles in the known universe'*. He recounts the tale of a spiritual master who ruled a small but prosperous domain, the boundaries of which began to expand.[35] He trained a number of emissaries, who became necessary to help manage the more distant parts and keep the population safe. Eventually, the most trusted of these, the cleverest and most ambitious, seeing his benevolence as weakness, grew contemptuous of his master. Usurping his position, he then began ruling as a tyrant, so that the people became miserable and the domain eventually collapsed in ruins. McGilchrist uses this story as an allegory, arguing persuasively that in modern culture, the master (the

---

35. Iain McGilchrist (2009) *The Master and his Emissary: The Divided Brain and the Making of the Western World*. New Haven and London: Yale University Press, p 14

right brain) has been deposed by its trusted emissary (the left brain) resulting in destructive imbalance.

The two halves – left and right – are connected to each other by a band of between 300 million and 800 million fibres, the *'corpus callosum'*, yet only about 2 per cent of neurones in the cerebral cortex on each side are linked by these fibres. Furthermore, it turns out that many of the connections in this transverse bundle are inhibitory, and designed specifically to stop the other hemisphere from interfering. Thus, to a considerable extent, the two half-brains are capable of operating separately, in parallel. They are structurally similar, but have significant differences of emphasis and function and here is a paradox: although they work independently, they continuously maintain some contact with each other. Simultaneously, in other words, they work both separately and together. In ideal circumstances, they function as one, a fully harmonised duality working as a united whole.

According to the principle of contralaterality, the left side of the brain controls the right side of the body and vice-versa. Although brain organisation varies from individual to individual, there is considerable consistency regarding both left-right distribution of hand-dominance and the opposite-side location of the speech area.

That the speech centres of the brain are in only one hemisphere forms part of a design in which the left brain deals with 'parts', with pieces of information in isolation. In contrast, the right brain deals with whatever is under consideration as a 'whole'. The left is well-suited to binary thinking, and the right to unitary experience. The silent right brain is attuned to whatever is new, while the speech-capable left depends rather upon what is familiar. In order to appreciate things whole and in their context, the right hemisphere consistently exhibits breadth and flexibility of attention, like a floodlight, compared to the focused intensity of which the left is more capable, like a spotlight.

According to McGilchrist, the human brain must attend to the world in two different ways at once:

In one (the right hemisphere) we experience the live, complex, embodied, world of individual, always unique beings, forever in flux, a net of interdependencies, forming and reforming wholes, a world with which we are deeply connected.

In the other (the left hemisphere) we 'experience' our experience in a special way: a 're-presented' version of it, containing now static, separable, bounded, but essentially fragmented entities, grouped into classes, on which predictions can be based. This kind of attention isolates, fixes and makes each thing explicit by bringing it under the spotlight of attention. In doing so it renders things inert, mechanical, lifeless. But it also enables us for the first time to know, and consequently to learn and to make things.[36]

There are, therefore, two corresponding kinds of 'knowing': knowing *about* things, using the left brain; and a more intimate and personal kind of knowing, using the right. For example, everyone 'knows about' clay, what it is and can be used for; but only a skilled potter or sculptor 'knows' clay well enough, through extensive personal experience, to become one with it and use it, almost as living matter, to create a distinctive object; a simple bowl perhaps, that is both useful and beautiful at the same time.

The two halves of the human brain thus bring two different types of world into being. The left brain has been found to prefer whatever is mechanical, impersonal and abstract. Associated with right hand dominance, as well as the seat of speech and language, it is concerned with making and using tools and machines. The right brain, in contrast, which sees nothing in the abstract, only things in context, takes primary

36. Ibid., p 31.

interest in what is living and personal. Appreciating things as whole, it is responsible for recognising that faces are faces, and as such human, not just juxtapositions of disconnected eyes, nose, mouth and so on, as the left brain would see them. It therefore recognises people as individuals, a sign of which is our remarkable capacity to appreciate even extremely rapid changes of facial expression.

The evidence firmly suggests that all forms of emotional perception, and most forms of emotional expression, depend on and inform the right hemisphere. This side of the brain is therefore central to satisfactory social interactions, and to those functions and abilities that enable human beings to form bonds; bonds of both attachment (of affection and love) and aversion (of dislike and hatred); through emotional understanding and interplay. The right brain, by extension, is also the seat of morality and a sense of justice. As McGilchrist points out, stimuli related to fellow-feeling and co-operation capture the master's right-brain attention, while those related to rivalry and competition are treated in preference by the emissary on the left.

As well as empathy, arrived at through identifying with others, the right hemisphere is also concerned with self-awareness, imagination, creativity and intuition. On it depend a number of intrinsically human capacities: the love of poetry, for example, fascination with metaphor, and the enjoyment of stories, especially illustrative stories such as allegories, fables and parables. Humour, including irony, satire and sarcasm, is also mediated via the right brain as it depends on understanding the context of what is said and done. The right brain alone can recognise and take delight in ambiguity and paradox, double and even triple meanings. Also, unlike the intolerant left, the right brain lives contentedly with change and uncertainty.

In complete contrast, a dominant left hemisphere, without the moderating influence of the right, results in dehumanisation, in people who may listen but cannot understand; who look but cannot really see. The left brain mediates only the more superficial social forms of emotional expression: the perfunctory smile of acknowledgement, for example, the slight shrug or almost imperceptible raising of the eyebrows.

The left brain is so averse to uncertainty and doubt that it can often cope only by arbitrarily picking just one interpretation as correct. Capable solely of binary (either/or, right/wrong) thinking, it is impatient with all other possibilities, which it construes therefore as wrong. The left brain thus commonly insists it is right, even when mistaken and in the face of evidence. Of the commoner emotions, it notices only anger, so frequently employed to defend the indefensible, a potent but misguided basis for the insistent feeling of 'being in the right'. According to McGilchrist, the left hemisphere supports only, '*A blanket disregard for the feelings, wishes, needs and expectations of others'*.[37] This obviously causes serious problems, conflict and suffering as a result.

Perhaps surprisingly, the left brain is unadventurous. It prefers what is familiar, only discovering more of what it already knows and doing more of what it is already doing. It avoids what is new, unfamiliar and strange. In contrast, the right hemisphere actively prefers what is new. It is constantly vigilant for change and anomalies. The remedy for an over-bearing left hemisphere therefore involves a powerful corrective influence from the right. Only the right brain can fully grasp the full interplay of the myriad of influences at work in a given situation.

The whole brain therefore needs to be in play for full understanding to be achieved. Wisdom – knowing how to be and behave for the best, for all concerned, in any given situation – while valuing the workings of the left brain, depends particularly on a balance between the two, governed in the final analysis by the right.

---

37. Ibid., p 58.

With the two hemispheres functioning similarly while running on markedly different agendas, there is an apparently perpetual tension or dissonance between the two. The tension can be reduced, however, particularly through a range of practices to be discussed in Chapter 15. The most notable in this context is 'meditation' (also referred to as 'mindfulness', 'stilling', or 'silent prayer'), during which left hemisphere activity calms right down, allowing promptings from the normally quiet right hemisphere to break through.

* * *

6

THE 'EVERYDAY EGO' AND THE 'SPIRITUAL SELF'

A number of authorities have referred to a powerful split at the heart of human psychology. One pioneer thinker in this field, Carl Jung, used the terms 'Ego' and 'Self'. Thomas Merton and others have written about the 'False Self' and the 'True Self'. Others speak of a 'worldly' self and a 'higher' self or 'soul'. Because also used in previous publications, the preferred terms in this book are the *'Everyday Ego'* and the *'Spiritual Self'*. [38]

According to the child psychiatrist and researcher, Donald Winnicot, there resides in newborn infants, *'a component of self which possesses a purity, wholeness, untarnished innocence and spontaneity'*,[39] which he referred to as their *'pristine ego'*. Unaffected by attachments and aversions, it is short-lived, however. In the face of urgent and immediate needs; for food, warmth, comfort, safety, affection, etcetera, the early infant ego soon finds itself faced with multiple

---

38. See Larry Culliford (2011) *The Psychology of Spirituality: an introduction,* London: Jessica Kingsley Publishers and (2015) *Much Ado About Something: a vision of Christian maturity,* London: SPCK.
39. Quoted in Victor Schermer (2003) *Spirit and Psyche: a new paradigm for psychology, psychoanalysis and psychotherapy.* London and New York, Jessica Kingsley Publishers,p 67.

conflicts and anxieties. Identifying completely with its own body, it soon feels pain, discomfort, frustration, abandonment and emptiness, to the point of insatiability.

This is the early origin of the split between the 'everyday ego' and the 'spiritual self'. Such an apparently binary formula, though, hides the reality that *they remain permanently connected*, forming an indivisible unity. Just as a length of elastic, or a guitar string, set in motion, appears to occupy more than one place at a time, due to its rapid fluctuations back and forth, so it is with the apparent dissonance between these two aspects of a person's selfhood. As the arc of life proceeds towards maturity, the apparent split initially grows wider, through the early stages of spiritual development described in Chapter 3. Later, during 'Individual' Stage 4, it starts to slow, beginning its homecoming reversal during 'Integration' Stage 5, and completing the re-unification process in the final 'Universal' Stage 6.

Diagram 1 (p. 70) gives a stylised version of the degree of tension and dissonance that develops and reduces again between the 'everyday ego' and the 'spiritual self' as a person goes through the six stages of spiritual growth. People who are inherently more mature, it seems, experience less tension than do others. The 'high', 'medium' and 'low' trajectories in the diagram indicate that, as life proceeds, some people experience less in the way of inner conflict, and make developmental progress through the stages more smoothly than others. Innate factors regarding one's temperament, together with aspects of personal conditioning as determined by one's social and familial spiritual environment, will be factors determining the general trend for each individual.

As the diagram also indicates, life events and experiences play an important role whenever 'something happens' of a deeply significant and personal nature to shift a person from a lower towards a higher trajectory or vice versa.

Consider, for example, how a child, raised with a simple Christian belief in the biblical Jesus capable of healing miracles, may have that faith weakened by an introduction to the

Diagram 1: Six Stages of Spiritual Development[40]

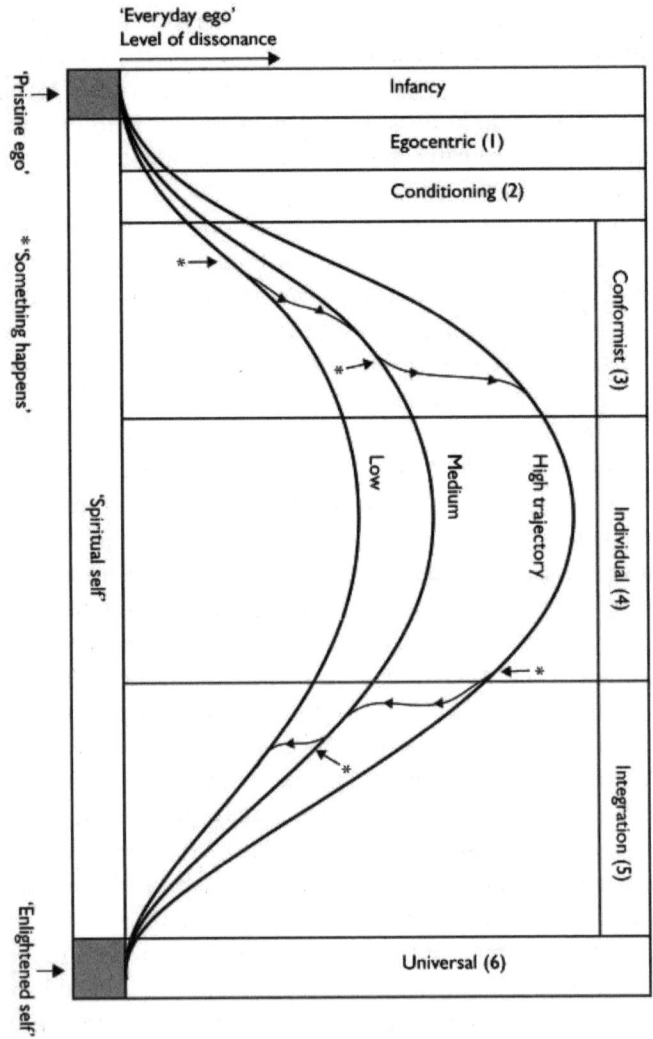

40. From Larry Culliford (2011) *The Psychology of Spirituality: an introduction*,
London: Jessica Kingsley Publishers p 160.

principles of science at school. Further imagine that the child's adored parent dies of a painful and debilitating disease, with no healing miracle occurring despite intense prayer. The challenge to that child's belief system will be severe, as innocence becomes tarnished by the experience. Spiritual awareness becomes dulled, more easily ignored as the child's 'everyday ego' shifts to a higher trajectory, towards more worldly concerns.

Nevertheless, as the diagram's bottom line shows, the spiritual self is never fully extinguished, remaining an influence to account for the important possibility of later re-integration. Imagine now, for example, that the same child experiences, much later, a comforting vision or dream in which the image of the dead parent communicates lovingly that they are well, at peace and free of pain. This is not unrealistic. Both Thomas Merton[41] and former US President Barack Obama[42] have recorded powerful and meaningful dreams or visions about their dead fathers, occurring when they were young adults. In both cases, the episode was followed by an intense bout of crying, this catharsis being followed by a gradual but permanent and more wholesome change in the direction of their lives and ambitions. Whenever 'something happens' like this to reduce the dissonance between 'true' and 'false' selves, a person's developmental trajectory is spontaneously lowered and readiness to pay attention to one's inner spiritual awareness is rekindled. The consequences usually show themselves clearly in terms of a healthy change in attitudes and values, of general demeanour, of patterns of speech and behaviour.

* * *

41. Thomas Merton (1948) *The Seven Storey Mountain*, p 123.

42. Barack Obama (2008) *Dreams from my Father*, London: Canongate, pp 128-129.

The 'everyday ego' is the *'me'* people experience most of the time, the personal self that, from birth, interacts with mother, father, siblings, the wider family and the social group at community, cultural, national and global levels throughout life. People are engaged both with their surroundings and with the world of inner experience. Through this ego, people form attachments and allegiances, also aversions. They develop likes and dislikes concerning people, places, objects, activities, sensations, ideas, ideologies, and all manner of things, including much that is created solely by the imagination.

Driven by the brain's left hemisphere, the everyday ego tends towards being self-centred, unadventurous, materialistic and possessive. Dominated rather by the right hemisphere, the 'spiritual self', in contrast, is naturally more selfless, creative, intuitive, humble, compassionate and wise. A stranger to desire, it does not form attachments or aversions. Dwelling in the moment, accepting the way things are, it has no sense of lacking anything for itself, while at the same time acknowledging, sharing, and seeking to remedy the many sufferings of others.

The 'spiritual self' is like the *'little point of nothingness'* referred to by Thomas Merton, seamlessly connected to the wider spiritual dimension of being, to the divine totality, the cosmic whole, to the Sacred Unity that some call 'God' or Holy Spirit, through which each person is connected to everyone else, to everything, throughout the universe and throughout time. Developing maturity therefore involves allowing one's true self to reveal itself, discovering and learning to inhabit it to an increasing degree, thereby revealing it to others. It therefore means becoming more conscious of what is happening moment by moment, developing greater discernment; having in this way both more choices and the opportunity to be more deliberate in terms of sensible, considered speech and action; equally, in refraining from unwise, hurtful behaviour. The pinnacle of spiritual development during Stage 6 thus involves a final merging or re-integration of 'everyday ego' and 'spiritual self' in the formation of an 'enlightened' or 'higher' being. There will be more about this again later.

* * *

7

BALANCING
CONFLICTING VALUES

Just as it is possible to describe tension, firstly between two ways of thinking, mediated by the two hemispheres of the human brain, also between the 'everyday ego' and the 'spiritual self', so is it possible to describe two sets of contrasting, often conflicting, sets of values: 'worldly', on one hand, and 'spiritual' on the other. The former, summarised by the notions of *power* and *possessions*, are those most associated with the left brain and the false, 'everyday ego'. The latter, summarised by the idea and ideals of *unconditional love*, associated with a dominant right brain, are brought to life through the influence of the true 'spiritual self'.

Attachment is at the heart of worldly values: the owning of property and possessions, having power and controlling people. Luxury, wealth and fame follow closely. Such values fuel personal and collective aims and ambitions. They are not, in themselves, to be condemned. Worldly success as a result of skill, hard work and determination is often praiseworthy. Nevertheless, as already discussed in Chapter 1, when worldly values override spiritual ones, suffering is the result.

Some points are worth repeating here. Success 'at all costs' leads to a culture dominated by secular materialism, mercenary commercialism and ever-expanding consumerism, which necessarily encourage partisanship and rivalry, and therefore inequality and conflict. A worldly attitude involves perpetually seeking opportunities; situations to be exploited for expansion and profit, for example, also opportunities to take and remain in control somewhere, often at the expense of other people. This is seen as admirable by those in the ascendant during 'Conformist' Stage 3, but comes under question, and is ultimately rejected, with increasing personal and spiritual maturity in the later stages.

From a psychological perspective, a primary (often unconscious) underlying motive for preferring worldliness over spirituality involves a strong element of evasion, denial and rejection of any form of personal suffering: physical, emotional, social and spiritual. Keeping one's left-brain spotlight on 'power', 'success', 'profit' and 'progress' avoids the need to acknowledge, much less take responsibility for, whatever havoc and distress might be visible using the much broader beam of one's right-brain floodlight. This is an example of immaturity.

Mature, spiritual values, on the other hand, embody both wisdom and compassion. They are noble values that arise with a natural human capacity for love, kinship and fellow feeling. They represent the truth at the heart of 'Integration' and 'Universal' Stages 5 and 6 that, to quote Thomas Merton again, *We are all already one*, that each person is seamlessly connected through the spiritual dimension to every other person, past, present and future.

Spiritual values therefore include the following:

- honesty
- trust
- kindness
- generosity
- tolerance
- restraint
- patience

- perseverance
- joy
- humour
- humility
- gratitude
- dignity
- devotion
- forgiveness
- courage
- compassion
- wisdom
- beauty
- hope

These values reflect supreme mental health, and only when such wholesome attributes prevail within a family, community, society or culture, can it be said to be fully healthy. When these values dominate, suffering is much reduced, in particular through being shared, diffused and diluted.

Living in the world in the ordinary way, this ideal involves a balancing act. A person advertising or selling goods, for example, must balance honesty and generosity with the requirement to promote their wares. It is easier to remain truthful, and to set a fair price, if what you offer is useful, of good quality, robust and genuinely attractive. It is easier to serve others, and profit the community as well as oneself, if you take the trouble to listen patiently, find out what people really need and provide only that, rather than offering products or activities that are unnecessary, may be destructive, could risk addiction, for example, or cause harm in any number of other ways.

The values in the above list all go together, being inherent in a person's true nature. Compassion, for example, is not a choice. It is built in to the 'spiritual self', attuned – consciously or otherwise – to the suffering of others, as revealed to me years ago. Here is the story.

As a trainee, I was deeply concerned about a psychiatric patient whose emotionally painful condition had not been responding to treatment and care. I spoke of it to a wise man, one of my teachers, who asked me first where the pain was located. 'In that terrible locked ward', I said, 'Where all the patients are suffering'. But he asked me again, 'Where is the pain, Larry?' The kindness in his voice made me see. 'Ah!' I exclaimed. 'It's here', I said, pointing to my own heart. 'And why does it hurt?' he asked. I was uncertain, and remained silent until he gave me the answer: 'It hurts because you care'.

This was helpful. It changed things for me. No longer was my suffering something to try and get rid of by foolishly thinking I might succeed where others had failed with this or any other patient in their distress. To cure his pain, even if it could be done, would not change the essential nature of mine – compassion – which was something to accept, an integral part of who I was; an attribute to reflect upon and learn through, rather than suppress. This new insight gave a valuable boost to my sense of self-worth. I am very grateful, both to that patient and to the teacher, who happened to be a Buddhist monk. The encounter gave me the wisdom to be realistic in my aims; to put my professional training and energy where it would do most good. Yet this did not mean neglecting the less fortunate, beyond the adequate reach of medicine and psychiatry, because now, free from the emotional burden, lifted by the monk's generous and insightful intervention, I could spend at least a little time sharing the patient's distress without inflicting further unnecessary ineffective treatment upon him, and without feeling unduly bad within myself. This sympathetic sharing of suffering seems to help.

During the immature stages of spiritual development, understandably but regrettably, a choice is often made by people to ignore their inner drive for compassion. This is where I was before I understood that to do so was futile. The new task was not to suppress compassionate instincts, but to pay attention to them, and manage them with as much wisdom as I could muster. This was a turning point for me.

* * *

PART TWO
Commentary

Things You May Want To Think About

'When someone whom I have assisted
And in whom I have placed great hope
Inflicts me with extremely bad harm,
I shall view him as my supreme spiritual friend.'[43]

43. Geshe Rabten, Geshe Ngawang Dhargyey (1977) *Advice from a Spiritual Friend,*
New Delhi: Publications for Wisdom Culture, p 17.

INTRODUCTION TO PART TWO

There is an ongoing debate about 'nature' and 'nurture', trying to decide which is more important regarding who a person turns out to be: what they inherit biologically from their parents through the DNA in their genes or the experiences they have during childhood and adolescence. From the wisdom perspective, arguing about this is unnecessary, because both factors are recognised as coming heavily into play.

Children during 'Conditioning' Stage 2 are very malleable, absorbing the life lessons and living examples of their parents and other teachers, both formal in schools and informal in the community. It is during later childhood and the teenage years that we begin to exert a measure of personal control and decision-making about the kind of person we wish to be and become. This is usually therefore a time of exploration and experimentation. Leaving home (for work, further education or on a 'gap year', for example) offers both challenges and opportunities for self-discovery through encountering new conditions and people who are culturally different. This may force us to re-examine the assumptions, allegiances, belief systems and values we have been living by until this point.

To clarify further the tasks and challenges involved in the earlier stages of spiritual development, here is a parable, which is to say a narrative of imagined events designed to convey a moral or spiritual message. It is the story of someone who left home out of curiosity, and his friend who remained behind.

Two men once lived with their tribe in a deep gorge, tucked into the slopes of a steep mountain range close by the ocean. The geography of the place was such that clouds and a dense layer of mist hung perpetually over the steep-sided valley. The people dwelling there seldom encountered direct sunlight, living out their lives in humidity, twilight and gloom.

One day, one of the young men made his way to a high peak, and momentarily caught a glimpse of sunlight striking the rock face. He felt its warmth on his skin. This was very rare, and the experience changed him. He began to question in his mind what had happened. When he asked others, including his parents and the tribal elders, they said it must have been a dream or an illusion; yet he knew himself to have been awake and in his right mind.

The certainty of the experience of light and warmth from the sun stayed with him, and he soon found himself wondering if the elders and tribal folklore could be mistaken in other ways. The rituals, directed by his tribe towards a deity they prized for keeping them hidden and safe in their cloud-covered valley, began to lose meaning for him. He began to prize clear-headed thinking over the tribe's routine practice of imbibing powerful narcotic intoxicants during their rituals.

The youth took to spending time alone, away from the tribal village, so that he could think for himself without interruption or distraction. He returned frequently to the hilltop where he had had his life-changing vision. Others in the tribe, especially from his family, noticed this change in behaviour, and began to encourage him to rejoin and recommit himself to group activities. The elder women said it was time for him to choose a wife. The men said he should be given his own dwelling and land, so he could start growing crops for himself. When he resisted, requesting patience, members of the tribe began thinking of him as strange. Some grew angry and impatient with him. He was pressing uncomfortably against invisible and long-accepted boundaries of attitude and conduct.

Apart from his friend who stayed loyal, the young man felt increasing discomfort among his own people, and with it a rising curiosity for an explanation about his experience on the hilltop. He decided to make a journey. Whatever the risks, he felt he must take them or never again know inner peace. This had happened before. A man had left the tribe approximately once in every generation, but none had ever returned.

After much discussion, the man managed to persuade his loyal friend to leave the security of the tribe and accompany him. Eventually, they set off on their pilgrimage, having to climb steeply, travelling inland over high passes through similar valleys for several days. The friend's disquiet grew with the distance travelled, intensifying until, during a fierce thunderstorm, his resolve gave way. He had grown terribly afraid, and now insisted on returning to the tribe where he was welcomed back with rejoicing.

Saddened, the first youth carried on, all the more determined to conquer his doubts and difficulties. Eventually, cresting a final peak, he came upon a watercourse flowing away from his tribal land towards the plain below. He followed it down, and by nightfall of the following day had reached even ground.

Waking the next morning, the traveller was struck by the clear sky, the dry air, the bright sunlight, the brilliance of the colours around him, and the pleasant if unaccustomed force of the heat. It brought immediate joy to his heart, and a sense of validation, a calming of his earlier doubts and fears.

Travelling on, he met the local people. To his surprise and pleasure, they spoke a similar language and looked like his own people, although – the climate being warmer – their skins were a shade darker and they dressed differently, wearing more colourful clothing of lighter material. They offered him food, and he noticed some differences here too. There were delicious fruits growing locally that he had not seen or tasted before. There was a greater variety of crops, and animals had been domesticated for farming, rather than having to be hunted or trapped.

Above all, the youth noticed how much more cheerful the people he encountered were, compared with his own people. They were welcoming and friendly. Their smiles made the young women seem to him more attractive. He could understand why no-one ever went back to the dark valley from which he had come.

Life was so much better in the bright daylight. The man in exile from his own tribe found work on a farm, and felt increasingly comfortable there. Nevertheless, he remembered his family and friends, feeling an irrepressible responsibility towards them. In due course, after several months, he made up his mind to return and tell them what he had found. He wanted to persuade some at least to follow him back, to take the risk of leaving the valley and share in a much better life. The independent-minded man, a youth no longer, said farewell to his new friends on the sunlit plain and retraced his steps. Fearless now, the return journey did not seem so hard. He simply followed the watercourse back up into the mountains, returning over the high passes to the cloud-covered valley of his tribe.

Among the first people he met was his former loyal friend. He was happy to see him, but his friend acted strangely, feeling ashamed at having abandoned him on the hillside. He was confused by the young man's joy. Expecting reproach, he barely recognised the smiling soul in front of him. He was bewildered by the darker shade of his skin and his colourful clothing and so he mistrusted his words.

"The sun shines every day on the plain", the returning pilgrim was saying. "Everyone is happy and content. There is so much life, so much vivid colour. The crops grow in abundance. The animals grow fat. There is enough for all to share. The people are very well fed, and they are very friendly. Life is much less of a struggle."

He asked his friend to have courage and return to the

plain with him, insisting that the journey was perfectly safe. "Please join me," he said. "We will return later, and together will persuade others to make the journey. Perhaps we can resettle everyone and be hailed as heroes." But his friend was not persuaded by this entreaty, and grew even firmer in his decision to stay. Later in life, this man became one of the tribal leaders in his turn, and was eventually acclaimed their chief.

The young man remained in the tribal valley for several weeks. He grew desperate to change his friend's mind, but he only noticed himself growing frustrated and gloomy again. His friend could not conceive of and believe in the existence of a sunlit country where people lived calm, happy lives of friendship and contentment. He remained convinced that he would be better off in familiar surroundings.

The young man also spoke to his parents, brothers and sisters, and was soon asked to go and speak to the tribal elders. In each case, the response was the same. No-one wanted to make the journey over the mountains to the plain. Their minds were closed. "That is not for us", people told him. "We have our ways, the ways of our ancestors. We belong here."

Sometimes the young man pleaded with his relatives. Sometimes he grew impatient and angry with the intransigence of the elders. Sometimes he even began to doubt his own experience of the world outside the valley, and sometimes he felt saddened, guilty and ashamed at the distress he was causing others whom he loved. He did not want to leave them, but felt increasingly alien among them. He again began spending time alone. He was confused and bewildered. He needed more time, and freedom from distraction, to think.

Eventually the young man came to understand that, in his heart, he had outgrown his tribe and its ways. He could not convert any among them to see matters his way. He felt shunned by the elders, who remained steadfastly indifferent to the outside world and intolerant of his message. They seemed close to branding him an outcast, as someone dangerous, a polluter of ancient tribal wisdom.

Unable to identify fully with his people, the youth decided to leave his tribe once again, returning to the sunlit plain below. He never went back. He had, however, sown some powerful seeds. Although he was never to know it, his actions did have positive consequences. Tribal children from future generations heard the stories about a young man who left, returned with tales of wonder from the plain, and went away again. Some were inspired to follow in his footsteps, to go and see for themselves. Later, some of these also made their way back to the tribe to confirm the earlier reports of an easier and happier life to be had elsewhere. Others eventually followed. There was finally a great exodus from the valley, with large numbers of the tribe's people relocating and integrating with the communities on the plain, taking their animals with them. A remnant, comprised mainly of older people left behind, withered quickly. In time, the shaded valley was left empty. Only a few carved wooden totems and ruined stone buildings remained.

* * *

This story emphasises, firstly, the strong interactions between individuals and the communal groups to which they belong during 'Conditioning' Stage 2 and 'Conformist' Stage 3, during which attachments, threats and losses, priorities and values operate at both personal and group levels, and shows that these may be at odds with each other. In this case, tribal attachments to traditional beliefs and practices were threatened by the young man's curiosity and his attachment to liberty, his desire to follow the prospect of an easier, happier, more interesting way of life.

The story demonstrates, too, how a single experience (that of sunlight for the youth) can bring about a universal realignment of someone's thinking and way of being, can ignite a passionate quest for a new vision of reality, a new truth, setting someone off on a kind of pilgrimage. This is the nature of spiritual awakening, at least for some people, setting them apart from the parent group, moving them along into 'Individual' Stage 4 and beyond. For others, it is a more gradual process, like those future generations of the tribe, influenced little by little by the folklore surrounding the first youth's adventures.

The parable shows that during 'Conformist' Stage 3, a person adheres to the culture, authority, values, belief system, rituals and other established behavioural practices of the family and communal group, in this case the tribe. Degrees of difference are tolerated, often encouraged, so that each new generation has a way of distinguishing itself from those that precede it. Nevertheless, there remains a degree of conformity about the new differences. Real challenges to the old order are much less well tolerated and usually resisted energetically. The threat to long and strongly held attachments, and therefore to communal stability, is experienced by the majority as unacceptably great.

The significance for the individual is consequential. The drive to belong to a group and retain the security this affords now appears to be in direct contrast to another powerful drive, to be more independent and think things through for oneself. Entering 'Individual' Stage 4 involves recognising this, and beginning to work out for oneself the ideal balance between the two. It means being torn between exploring the new territory and staying behind where all is familiar and feels safe. This is not simply an academic exercise. A person has to travel around in the new country, to investigate its similarities and differences, and to live by the new conventions in different circumstances. Simply to use one's imagination to think about what the new place might be like is inadequate, it being so easy to conjure up a picture that is in some, perhaps many, ways false.

Whatever the new environment is like, going away from home into another territory involves loss. It involves leaving places, people and other attachments behind. As described in

Chapter 4, the emotions of loss on occasions like this often include bewilderment, doubt, anxiety, anger, shame and guilt, before sadness supervenes, heralding healing, recovery and a return to calm, confident, joyful, contented acceptance of the changes involved.

The people left behind also feel naturally aggrieved, and are subject to a similar set of painful emotions, but with less likelihood of relief. Living with small, partial certainties prevents individuals and groups alike from having the complete 'holistic' vision required for completion of the emotional healing process which also brings spiritual growth.

Some elements of contemporary society remain 'tribal' in the sense that strong attitudes of conformism prevail in politics, religion, economics and other fields of human activity and enterprise. This may be particularly true under totalitarian political or military regimes. The same kind of tensions between groups of people, and challenges for the individual, remain everywhere.

* * *

Given that most adults in industrial society are thought to be at Stage 3, Stage 4, or oscillating between the two, it is worth trying to clarify the situation using another metaphor: that of spacecraft and the effects of gravity.

When parent groups and communities, such as the tribe in the above parable, insist rigidly on conformity from its members, the gravitational pull is strong, so huge amounts of energy are needed to escape. The friend left his earth-bound tribe like an under-powered spaceship, only to fall back again, whereas the young man made good his escape into orbit. This is the first requirement, to get far enough away to gain a new perspective, have time to reflect, spy out patterns and discover alternatives.

Present-day astronauts commonly report a change in vision and personal attitude regarding life on earth once they return from space. For example, in 1971, as his spaceship travelled back amidst the vast darkness of the cosmos, his eyes fixed on the majestic blue sphere we call home, Dr. Edgar Mitchell, the sixth person to walk on the moon, was enveloped by a profound sense of universal connectedness. It changed him permanently. On his return to earth, Mitchell explained, *'I realized that the story of ourselves as told by science — our cosmology, our religion — was incomplete and likely flawed. I recognized that the Newtonian idea of separate, independent, discrete things in the universe wasn't a fully accurate description. What was needed was a new story of who we are and what we are capable of becoming.'*

Mitchell's transformative experience led him to establish the Institute of Noetic Sciences in 1973. [44] He understood that by applying the same scientific rigour used in the exploration of outer space, we could better understand the mysteries of inner space — the space in which he felt an undeniable sense of interconnection and oneness. [45]

More recently, people visiting the International Space Station orbiting Earth have had similarly powerful experiences. Astronaut Chris Hadfield, for example, is recorded as saying, *'One of the greatest changes I noticed within myself as a result of flying in space was that the difference between 'Us' and 'Them' disappeared. Somehow going round the world in 92 minutes, not just once but over and over and over again, turned the world into one shared place. I think it's a perspective that seeps into astronauts. I think it's a perspective that's kinda good for everybody.'*

In the same television documentary,[46] Leland Melvin said, *'I truly believe if more and more people could have*

---

44. See Appendix 2 for website details.

45. Dr Mitchell can be heard describing his experience at:

https://noetic.org/about/origins, accessed 11th September 2019.

46. *One Strange Rock*, episode 10, shown originally on the National Geographic Channel. See Appendix 2 for website details on how to view it.

the opportunity to see the planet from space, looking at the rich colours, looking at the fact that there are no borders separating us, we could see that we are all connected as human beings'.

* * *

The young man first left home with his outlook changed, but he still felt compelled to go back to the dark valley. Only later, fuelled by spiritual energy garnered from the sun, from his unhappy encounters within his own tribe, and from much better experiences with the people of the sunshine plain, did he gather sufficient momentum to escape permanently, like a spacecraft reaching escape velocity, bursting out of orbit, heading for the moon, the outer solar system, and further, towards liberation and the magnificent infinity of the universe, a reality beyond all imagination. This represents for us a model of spiritual growth.

* * *

8

POLITICS

The original book, 'Seeking Wisdom', was completed shortly after the UK Brexit referendum in 2016. Part Two of the present updated and expanded volume is being revised in the final weeks before the current Brexit deadline, 31st October 2019. European politics is changing, and the UK is currently in stalemate with no apparent way forward. It is possible that readers will find what follows both prescient and increasingly relevant. The sets of ideas presented in Part One are used in the following chapters with the aim of providing clarity, also hope.

* * *

Under totalitarian societies, old-style monarchies, military dictatorships, fascist regimes, socialist and communist state systems, an authoritarian style of government operates. Institutions are subordinate to the ruling body, which similarly demands the complete subservience of individuals. This approach typifies that of 'Conditional' Stage 2 and 'Conformist' Stage 3 thinking, while being severely intolerant of 'Individual' Stage 4 impulses. They work, and work well for many thousands of people, but only up to a point. Because they restrict human psychological impulses to think, speak, act and take responsibility for oneself, systems like this can be said to contravene the natural order of things. To combat individualism, totalitarian rulers tend to grow increasingly repressive, unjust and dictatorial. In doing so, they risk fostering increasing levels of opposition, setting up a vicious cycle – more opposition, more repression and vice versa – leading to ongoing instability. Demonstrations against the political leadership are increasingly frequently reported, for example currently in Moscow and Hong Kong. The result is the reverse of what those leaders are usually seeking: the growth through adversity towards wisdom and maturity of the populace at the personal level.

In western cultures, the prevailing model of government involves a parliamentary democracy or similar party system, better suited to Stage 4 independence. Safeguards against political tyranny in the UK, for example, include the established existence of a constitutional monarchy, an upper house, a separate judiciary and legal system, and accountable law enforcement agencies. Such a system has been operating for a long time, and still seems adequate, representing an advanced degree of social maturity. Nevertheless, it is not without room for improvement.

The political scene is changing. In the UK, there are no longer two principal parties (Labour and Conservative) buffered by a third (Liberal Democrat), offering opposing options on various issues from which voters can choose. The situation is more complicated, reflecting a growing diversity of interests and interest groups. It is almost certainly influenced too by the increasing number of people moving from 'Conformist' Stage 3 of personal and spiritual development towards and into 'Individual' Stage 4. Whether from selfish or altruistic motives, more people wish to think important matters through independently, and therefore seek greater flexibility and choice.

One result has been a proliferation of political parties represented in the House of Commons, each with different values, attitudes and agendas.[47] There have always been vested interests, but now there are professional lobbyists and many powerful organisations with vast resources vying for the attention and support of different politicians and political groups. There is great risk of the political views and positions of individuals being overwhelmed and discounted by such factions, adding to the general tension in contemporary politics. When the individual vote is devalued in this way, democracy itself is threatened. People naturally feel aggrieved, but helpless in the face of limited options.

The maximum five-year life of a government also imposes significant imperatives, as, of course, does the necessity for politicians to gain and retain sufficient votes to hold power at local and national levels.

Although cross-party committees and occasional 'free' votes for Members of Parliament, unrestricted by party allegiances, allow for a degree of harmony, the prevailing mood and manner of British politics (as elsewhere, particularly throughout Europe and the Americas) is competitive, even combative. Drawing on the observations of neuroscience described in Chapter 5, this type of increasingly polarised and multi-faceted environment depends heavily on binary thought processes (on right/wrong, Us/Them thinking) involving left hemisphere driven, oppositional attitudes and modes of communication and behaviour: threatening, defamatory remarks and hostile tweets, for example.

* * *

In marked contrast, the wisdom view is deliberately unifying. Incorporating a more spiritual approach, it gives primacy to the individual perspective. In this, being guided by deep personal

---

47. In the 2017 UK General Election, representatives of the following parties were successful: Conservative, Labour, Liberal Democrat, Green, Co-operative, Scottish National, Democratic Unionist, Plaid Cymru, and Sinn Fein.

experience, it depends on right hemisphere mediated unitary, both/and style thinking. Importantly, wisdom acknowledges the principle of 'reciprocity', already mentioned in earlier chapters. It also recognises that, while trying to minimise it, a significant degree of human suffering is inevitable. The wisdom approach involves using this as fuel for personal spiritual development and, in the political context, also for communal growth towards social maturity.

The wisdom view looks purposefully at all angles, considering what is positive in a given situation alongside what is unsatisfactory, before advocating change. It can, when necessary, be decisive, knowing that immediate and sweeping measures are sometimes required in the face of impending catastrophe. It is, however, more often reflective, knowing that changes cause less disruption and suffering when introduced gradually over time.

The wisdom view, then, is patient. In taking the long-term perspective, it remembers that, where action is under consideration, three options are present, not two:

    a) to decide on a course of action;
    b) to decide to avoid a particular course of action;
    c) to wait.

A planned delay allows emotions to settle. Revisiting ideas from Chapter 4, the positive feelings of calm, clarity and acceptance emerge increasingly as fear, doubt, confusion and irritation settle. Waiting also allows time for those concerned to investigate the situation further and gain important relevant information in respect of decisions to be made. It allows room for intelligent, unbiased and informed discussion and the wider canvassing of opinion.

Furthermore, the wisdom view takes into account the intense cohesive power of institutions and systems of politics to assimilate even major shifts in circumstances and points of view. It encourages faith that, after a period of instability and uncertainty (such as after a landslide General Election, a significant referendum reversal, or a crash in the economy), the altered political landscape will eventually re-stabilise. Wisdom, based on fellow-feeling, understands that people are well-motivated to help each other get their lives back in order following misfortune.

Throughout any upheaval, political or otherwise, the human condition remains the same. Daily life continues, and people face the same challenges with which to cope, the same threats and losses to face and endure. Everyone must find a way to fulfil their needs and obtain the essentials: food, shelter, safety, education and health care among them. They must meet, too, their requirements for occupation, recreation, companionship and a sense of meaning, the feeling that life is worthwhile. The wisdom view considers all these needs paramount.

There are grounds for hope, too, when we consider the many enduring successes brought about under the present political system. In 1883, for example, the UK's Slavery Abolition Act was introduced, and in that year too Parliament began voting to provide sums of money annually for the construction of schools for poor children. The Elementary Education Act of 1880 insisted on compulsory school attendance for children from 5 to 10 years old. In 1972, the school leaving age was raised to 16, and the 1988 Education Reform Act introduced the National Curriculum. The UK National Health Service came into being in 1948, following an Act of Parliament two years earlier. These represent but a few of democracy's crowning achievements.

In aiming to benefit the greatest number of people, based on the principle of reciprocity, the wisdom view recommends giving the weaker and more disadvantaged members of society pride of place in all political deliberations. Failing to invest sufficiently in compassionate health and social care, for example, including the sympathetic management of criminal offenders, seems unwise, with a high consequent social cost in terms of additional and unnecessary suffering for all.

The converse of wisdom, which is folly, depends on a specific kind of ignorance, the ignorance of context, of the bigger picture; ignorance derived from the brain's impatient, arrogant, self-serving, narrow-vision, worldly left hemisphere in contrast to the more settled, altruistic, broad-vision, spiritual right. History has shown repeatedly, for example, that replacing one apparently flawed situation or system of government by another deemed better – through aggressive incursions, revolutions, map changes (e.g. partition), or through any other form of large-scale social engineering – alters but does not necessarily improve matters. In fact, history shows that such interventions often result in widespread disruption and suffering. Patience involving a gradual, well-informed approach, is usually wiser.

The quality of leadership matters in politics. It makes a difference whether leaders or leading groups adhere mainly to left-brain led worldly or right-brain influenced spiritual values, whether in other words they are dominated by *power* on the one hand, or *love* on the other. The issue of leadership is also relevant in the context of large organisations, both secular and religious, so this topic will be addressed separately in the following chapter.

* * *

9

LEADERS AND FOLLOWERS

There are several possible routes by which people arrive at positions of leadership in society: by inheritance, via promotion, through a selection procedure such as an election, or by using power and influence to impose oneself. Leaders tend to show different qualities according to the different stages of spiritual development. Similarly, people at the different stages seek different qualities in their leaders. Broadly speaking, the two can be mapped onto each other.

As a general principle, the more spiritually mature a person, the less likely she or he will be to seek the power and privilege of a leadership position. A combination of humility and wisdom holds such a person back. At the other end of the spectrum, it is dictators who impose themselves upon the world, seeking exactly that eminence. They commonly exhibit the attributes of a person stuck throughout adulthood in the primitive 'Egocentric' Stage 1, characterised by a deeply flawed, narcissistic sense of omnipotence, fierce intolerance of opposition, and a strong predisposition to feelings of persecution. They are dangerous because of their exceptionally limited capacity for empathy, unable directly to experience the emotional states of other people, rendering them capable of immense and unfeeling cruelty.

Nevertheless, such people attract followers in large

numbers. Those who, as adults, remain at the relatively unquestioning and involuntary 'Conditioning' Stage 2 tend to identify with the perceived strength and apparent self-confidence of such a leader, responding with both fear and excitement to repeated bullying threats and enthralling (but seldom delivered) promises, the sticks and carrots used by tyrants to achieve and remain in power.

People at 'Conformist' Stage 3 may also react positively to dictatorial leadership, but they are more conscious of the risks and benefits of supporting a new leader and regime. It is more of a choice for them than during the period of reflex decision-making which is Stage 2. Often of fragile self-esteem, people in Stage 3 remain keen to evade any risk of ostracism or punishment, seeking always to avoid exclusion, to belong. They are uncritically inclined therefore to latch onto the wave of public opinion and kowtow to its enforcers.

People at 'Individual' Stage 4, keen to think, speak and act independently, make more deliberate choices and can go either way; to support or oppose any new leadership. If it is obviously tyrannical and corrupt, some may rebel and offer resistance; others will seek to join the regime, without revealing their true, essentially self-centred loyalty, seeing the situation as an opportunity for personal gain.

People in the more mature 'Integration' and 'Universal' Stages 5 and 6 also face options: either to rise up selflessly in opposition to a merciless dictatorial regime, risking reprimand, expulsion, unjust retribution, incarceration, even martyrdom; or sagely to bide their time and avoid confrontation, helping the victims of tyranny where possible, remaining confident of a better future, thereby instilling courage and offering hope.

* * *

Dictatorship and military rule are more likely where democracy has not been established, or when it comes under threat. When democracy prevails, the more usual picture has been of a different quasi-conformist style of leadership. A traditional system involving two main political parties, with one main alternative, as in the UK's recent past, appeals notably to people in the earlier stages of spiritual development. It suits people comfortable with long-term allegiances, people who prefer to make their political decision once and for all. In the USA, for example, people might still openly declare themselves 'life-long' Democrats or Republicans. A measure of trust is involved that their views will in general coincide with the majority of other supporters and the party's leaders, and they may not yet be ready to acknowledge that this could be seen as an evasion of full personal responsibility for what happens. Under this system, while party allegiances remain relatively fixed, political leaders are relatively expendable; coming and going, depending largely on their popularity and the level of political success or failure with which they are associated.

As noted earlier, though, there is much less stability in politics these days. With increasing numbers of people world wide reaching 'Individual' Stage 4, there is a greater call everywhere for accountability among leaders from all the various political ideologies, from the toughest to the most liberal. People everywhere seek greater freedom and independence, broader choices, and much better opportunities to live creative and fulfilling lives, to use what they can offer to make a unique and valued contribution to society and the welfare of others.

This is difficult for leaders. Too liberal a stance will result in social chaos and an increasingly ungovernable populace. Too oppressive a reaction, on the other hand, will only stir up more resentment and fuel opposition. Even steering a middle path between the two will be difficult. This is because, at the outset of Stage 4, a person's concerns tend to remain principally self-interested. Caution is called for from everyone, because of the significant dangers associated with widespread 'individualism'; with a kind of 'we know better' attitude among a population seeking greater independence when the leadership is still expecting and insisting on discipline and obedience.

To avoid the risks of violent crackdown, on one hand, or un-governability and large-scale anarchy on the other, citizens will be obliged to develop a high degree of personal discipline and restraint, recognising that freedom automatically and necessarily brings responsibility. This is the wisdom of maturity. In the meantime, such increasingly independent-minded people require highly skilled leaders, able not only to recognise these tendencies, but capable also of fostering them as constructively as possible, in the knowledge that the many who depend on their judgements are simply following their true nature. They want what everyone wants: security, dignity, meaning, peace and plenty.

In such fragile and fractious political situations as prevail today, it seems wise for those in authority to be transparent and flexible, to provide timely information of good quality, and to demonstrate sound and universally sympathetic reasoning about important matters under consideration. It is clearly best to consider all possibilities and offer creative alternatives; to foster independent thinking and discussion on the topic; to listen to everyone involved, including both the powerful *and* the marginalised, while being prepared all along either to act decisively in everyone's best interest, to refrain from impetuous action for the sake simply of being seen 'to do something', or to encourage patience and wait, gather more information and consult more widely.

* * *

The political situations under dictatorships and totalitarian regimes, as well as in democracies, may be causing considerable frustration, even despair, among those affected. There does not seem to be any immediate prospect of enlightened change occurring anywhere soon. Nevertheless, from the wisdom perspective, there is hope, and this lies within individuals who will take the opportunities that an adverse predicament will provide to make progress on the path towards what psychology professor Reza Arasteh has called 'final personality integration',[48] equivalent in essence to spiritual maturity and wisdom. These are people with the ability to remain engaged within society while also detached in some measure, helped undoubtedly by both a well-developed sense of humour and a robust spirit of adventure. When the future is hard to predict with any degree of certainty, and thus hard to prepare for, we must expect the unexpected with fortitude. *'What cannot be remedied must be endured!'* as the saying goes.

Those who have already entered 'Integration' Stage 5 and 'Universal' Stage 6, would surely prefer political leaders to be at least as wise and mature as themselves. The wise have a natural aptitude for recognising wisdom and compassion – or the want of them – in those seeking political office; but they may be relatively unconcerned about *external* leadership within society, their focus being more on the *internal* leadership and guidance people can discover through paying close attention to the inherent wisdom of one's sacred inner compass or 'spiritual self' in tune with some form of cosmic unifying principle, a sacred universal breath or holy spirit. Dissatisfaction comes, in this way, to be regarded more as signalling an opportunity for personal growth than as a need for leadership action and external change.

* * *

48. A. Reza Arasteh (1975) *Toward Final Personality Integration: A Measure for Health, Social Change, and Leadership,* 2nd edition. New York and London: Wiley.

10

RELIGION

The scriptures and other wisdom literature of the world's major religions provide humanity with immense treasure troves, to be plundered freely; and yet they are treated with suspicion and consistently ignored by many. People may think that you have to be an acknowledged follower of a certain religion to benefit from its historical writings. The view of wisdom as being universal suggests that this is not the case. Such rejection of what is deemed 'other' comes from left-brain induced 'Conformist' Stage 3 attitudes. Religious wisdom literature is also often under-appreciated when people are influenced by 'Individual' Stage 4 thinking, seldom wanting to be told what to believe, and resentful at being preached at. Whether they think of themselves as 'spiritual' or otherwise, it is increasingly common to hear people say they are decidedly *not* religious.

In the earlier stages of spiritual maturity, it is hard to make the clear distinction between human spirituality and organised religion. As described in Chapter 3, spirituality is at the pinnacle of the 5-dimension hierarchy, and occupies a unifying position of personal and collective experience, whereas religions (through their institutions) are better considered as centred within the social dimension. Spirituality expresses the sacred unity of humankind and the cosmos. In contrast, there are many world religions, and within each several denominations, so the many different organisations tend to split people into groups and polarise them thoroughly.

The complex relationship between spirituality and the religions can be clarified using another metaphor, according to which spirituality can be thought of as the vital and nourishing central root of a great tree, while the major religions form its main branches. The lesser branches in turn can be imagined as representing smaller scale denominations of those religions and other faith traditions.

Supporters of religion, and religious organisations, point out that they have inspired many noble acts of self-sacrifice and altruism, stimulated great art and architecture, motivated people to develop moral and ethical systems, and been a guardian and force behind learning, health care, commerce and other major activities, with a remarkable legacy of universities, schools, hospitals and social welfare. One unifying suggestion here might be that the influence of the great, holy spirit-breath of the universe is at work through all the different religious organisations to bring about these highly valued events and developments. Many will wish to point out in addition, however, that religions do not hold a monopoly on good works. Secular institutions and their adherents have, in recent decades, rivalled religions in similar terms, indicating that atheist belief systems too can have their roots in the spiritual dimension. People who consider themselves *'spiritual but not religious'*, will have little difficulty going along with this.

In contrast, to even the balance, many people also choose to emphasise negative aspects of religion, for example that it has served as an ultra-conservative and repressive influence, has led to social and cultural divisions, and been the excuse for barbaric warfare, genocide, terrorism, torture and executions. At the personal level, it has resulted in psychological hardship and damage, a source of exaggerated guilt, shame, fear and anxiety. Dogmatic teaching within religious contexts on ways of thinking and behaving have hindered educational development, led to rigid and punitive styles of parenting, justified unfair and pernicious social stratification, led to unnatural and repressive attitudes towards the body and sexual relations, and hindered creative expression. From the wisdom perspective, however, this is not the fault of religions, as such, whose stated aims are uniformly directed towards human temporal and spiritual welfare. Much of it can better be ascribed to the immature, unwise and unnecessary insistence on conformity that some religious leaders and their followers are inclined to insist upon, coupled with the associated intolerant rejection of those who disagree with established belief systems, codes and culture. These problems can be counted on to fade as a result of growing maturity, humility, tolerance, compassion, wisdom and universal love.

In summary, the two sides of religion, destructive and creative, can be explained in terms of contrasting immature and mature spiritual development, from which people outside organised religion are by no means exempt. One researcher in America, for example, has described five types of *'spiritual-but-not-religious'* people according to their attitudes:

> *Dissenters* – critical of religion;
> *Casuals* – who consider spiritual practices as of value because leading mainly towards better health, stress relief and emotional support;
> *Explorers* – seeking novelty and new experiences without settling;
> *Seekers* – decidedly looking for a fresh spiritual home;
> *Immigrants* – in the pre-commitment process of adjusting to a new spiritual home or community.[49]

---

49. Linda Mercadante (2014) *Belief without Borders:Inside the Minds of the Spiritual but not Religious*, Oxford Scholarship Online.

Some religious organisations are relatively rigid in terms of their belief systems and faith practices, while others are more liberal. Nevertheless, all tend towards Conformism, exerting a powerful gravitational pull, seeking to attract people in big numbers and making it hard for followers to break away, either firstly into orbit around them, or more completely into the freedom of a clear conscience and open space.

In a secular culture, the fact that its mysteries face strong challenges from the findings of science makes it easier for people to turn their backs on religion. They may have started thinking independently of their religious upbringing, but for many the secular worldview has become the new focus of their conformism. In reaction, other individuals cling ever more tightly as adults to religious influences from their childhood, remaining Conformist too. Even those making genuine progress to Individual Stage 4 may not yet have grasped the possibility of making even further spiritual progress throughout life.

The Christian writer, Richard Rohr, for example, emphasises that *'the journey into the second half of our own lives'* awaits everybody. Calling this further journey a well-kept secret, of which too few are aware, he says that although everybody gets older, not everyone sets out on this second half of the pilgrimage, or makes it very far. *'People at any age must know about the whole arc of their life and where it is tending and leading'*, he writes.[50] The six stages guidance scheme hopefully makes it easier for people to get their spiritual bearings, and so help them make and carry out decisions in both halves of life.

According to Rohr, the first half of the journey involves 'surviving successfully'; by establishing an identity, home-base, family and friends, livelihood, regular pastimes and so on: the essential aspects of community and security. For

---

50. Richard Rohr (2012) *Falling Upward: a spirituality for the two halves of life*, London: SPCK, pp vii-viii.

the majority of people, this is all there is, valuing a sense of belonging, and prizing what is familiar and habitual. But Rohr criticises: *"Our institutions, including our churches, are almost entirely configured to encourage, support, reward, and validate the tasks of the first half of life. Most of us are never told that we can set out from the known and familiar to take on a further journey.'* [51]

In expressing his disappointment, Rohr makes clear that some people, even young people, do in contrast become aware of and accept the challenge to move forward, to escape the gravitational pull of conformity, to take responsibility and work towards spiritual maturity. Religious organisations, fearful of being outgrown and losing numbers, seldom appear to promote this. Brave people who think for themselves and ask questions, trying for example to square scientific discoveries with time-honoured spiritual teachings and truths, receive woefully inadequate encouragement and support. It seems natural, even admirable, when such a person turns away from organised religion and the religious teachers who fail them in this way.

The situation may change as religious leaders grow to understand the process better, attending more assiduously to their own spiritual development, growing wiser, more tolerant and flexible, encouraging independent-mindedness, letting people move away without considering it regrettable or a failure, and being better prepared to welcome such individuals back into active roles within the faith community when they are ready for re-integration and clearly working towards spiritual maturity.

Most world religions have already mapped well-trodden spiritual pathways, exemplified by the life journeys of mystics, saints and gurus. Holy men and women past and present have led the way: spiritual masters from Judaism, Christianity, Islam (notably Sufism), Buddhism, Hinduism,

---

51. Ibid., p xvii.

Sikhism, Taoism, Jainism and other traditions. Such wise and compassionate people have much in common, particularly the use of silence, stillness and solitude, also the practice of meditation, mindfulness, or silent prayer.

Solitude, incidentally, does not involve loneliness (of which many people have a terrible fear); quite the reverse. Loneliness involves painful emotional feelings of absence, of separation and loss. Solitude, in contrast, allows a person to settle into a comfortable, even joyful, state of 'being with oneself', a state that fosters a strong sense of connection and communication with others through the divine wind or holy spirit of the universe. Rather than empty, one's conscious awareness seems satisfyingly full; an experience that can be described, but must really be felt personally to be understood properly.

* * *

There is much to be learned too about spiritual maturity from elders and skilled practitioners of the ways and folklore of surviving indigenous populations.[52] In many tribal cultures, adolescent boys and girls are required to mature into adult members of their close-knit community; to become increasingly capable of independence of thought, word and action, and of taking responsibility, without either leaving the tribe or damaging its integrity. A system of 'initiation' enables this development, characterised by the learning of traditions, specific knowledge and skills, and by the facing of challenges. For the boys, these tend to be based mainly on hunting; for the girls, on childbirth. When completed successfully and fear conquered, the initiate is rewarded in a special ceremony, a 'rite of passage'.

52. See, for example, Kent Nerburn (2017) *Neither Wolf Nor Dog: on forgotten roads with an Indian Elder,* Edinburgh: Canongate and Erica M Elliott (2019) *Medicine and Miracles in the High Desert: My Life among the Navajo People,* Bloomington, Indiana: Balboa Press.

Until teaching and leadership on more advanced aspects of the spiritual path are better provided by a person's culture or religion, individuals in western society have no alternative but to seek wisdom elsewhere, taking responsibility for themselves. As the 'everyday ego' comes increasingly under the influence of the 'spiritual self', the inner imperative to do this grows accordingly. Life becomes akin to a pilgrimage, with an inherent sense of mission and the revival of a sense of honouring one's truest self.

It seems surprising that relatively few people living in a secular western culture reach such a turning point, going forward by making a personal commitment to seeking wisdom, when one considers the positive relationship of children to the spiritual dimension, as explored in the following chapter.

* * *

11

EDUCATION

Research into childhood spirituality was wrong-footed in the 1960s by an excessive intellectual bias. This changed only when researchers began listening to what the children actually said, without imposing their own interpretations on the narratives they heard and recorded. According to more recent research, though often invisible to the adult world, it is normal for most children to have rich and varied spiritual lives. Their experiences serve to underpin altruistic and ethical behaviour, guiding children towards enduring meaning, purpose and connectedness throughout life. Aspects of children's spirituality can also help when losses and other forms of adversity are encountered.

Children's spirituality is said to involve moments of reverence, awe, delight and wonder. It may concern the afterlife and life's ultimate questions; tends to include religious experiences; and may also involve a darker side of spiritual experience. David Hay and Rebecca Nye [53] were able to identify a common thread, a core category to which they gave the name, *'relational consciousness'*, similar to the idea of 'spiritual awareness'. The two main aspects of this category are:

---

53. David Hay & Rebecca Nye (2006) *The Spirit of the Child* (Revised Edition), London: Jessica Kingsley Publishers.

1. During private interviews with a specially trained researcher (Nye), the children demonstrated an unusual level of consciousness or perceptiveness, compared with during other passages of conversation.

2. The conversation was expressed in terms of four particular types of special quality relationship with:
   a. Things
   b. Other people
   c. The child himself or herself
   d. God

Here is six year old Ruth, described by Rebecca Nye as happy and articulate, with a profound sense of wonder and delight, who described attending Anglican Sunday School as boring, but imagined heaven like this:

> *A mist of perfume, with gold walls, and a rainbow stretched over God's throne... pervaded by a lovely smell, like the smell that you get when you wake up on a dull winter morning, and then when you go to sleep, and you wake up, the birds are chirping, and the last drops of snow are melting away, and the treetops, shimmering in the breeze, and it's a spring morning... It's not a season at all, not really, because it's just a day in delight, every day.* [54]

Another six year old, John, speaking to researcher Nye, told her how he 'sees' God:

> *With my mind and with my eyes. Sometimes I feel that... I am in a place with God in heaven and I'm talking to him... And there's room for us all in God. He's... God's... well, he is in all of us... He's in everything*

---

54. Ibid., pp 94-5.

that's around us. He's that microphone. He's that book.
He's even... He's sticks. He's paint. He's everything
around us... inside our heart... heaven. [55]

Older children were found to reflect more intentionally
on their thoughts, feelings and experiences, such that it was
often an *objective* insight into their *subjective* responses that
gave them a new dimension of understanding, meaning and
experience.

Hay and Nye found that many children are able to
develop a positive personal identity and sense of purpose
through awareness of being part of something far greater than
themselves. Some of the children seemed to have given up
their use of religious language and spiritual imagery because
it apparently failed to capture the inherent complexity and
mystery the children wanted to convey. The attempt was
therefore discarded. Instead, their spiritual awareness still
intact, they turned to other means of expression.

Numerous researchers have observed, however, that a
reduction in spiritual awareness and expression is normal in
industrialised societies among older children (above about 10
to 12 years). As they encounter religious scepticism and the
traditions of science, young people are under intense pressure
to conform to the prevailing secular worldview.

At 'Conditioning' Stage 2, children naturally respond to
the powerful influences and imperatives of families, teachers
and peer groups. It follows then that children's spiritual
awareness needs to be discovered, acknowledged and nurtured
if they are to grow into whole-minded people who are not
only cognitively, but also socially, emotionally and spiritually
developed. The catch is that some adults, those who are not
yet sufficiently spiritually mature themselves, may struggle
to recognise and encourage the spirituality of the children in
their care and sphere of influence.

---

55. Ibid., p 102.

As a result of this conditioned dampening, receiving limited encouragement, and having no adequate language of expression, awareness of the spiritual dimension fades and disappears from children's lives, almost to the point of vanishing, but seldom utterly and completely. The residue seems to go to ground, lying dormant unless and until 'something happens' to rekindle it. These observations have considerable significance, not only for the education of children, but also for the progress of adults towards spiritual maturity, a process likely to have stalled due to early and involuntary, secular conditioning.

Education (from the Latin *e-ducere*, meaning 'to lead out') involves helping children discover and bring forth knowledge and wisdom from within by fostering intuitive right-brain activity, rather than simply the imposition and learning of facts and skills in ways that rely solely on, and therefore develop mainly, left-brain functioning. Time for both reverie and play is, therefore, essential for the spiritual well-being of children, who need to reflect, play out and work through the many problematic issues that confront them, day by day. The most satisfactory curriculum therefore fosters a balance between learning facts and making sense of experiences; between left and right brain activity. Meditation, which harmonises left-right brain activity, is therefore valuable and recommended.

There is good evidence that children introduced in school to regular meditation (also called 'mindfulness' or 'stilling') even for very short periods once or twice daily, benefit through improvement in conduct, enhanced learning ability, creativity and imagination, and have better relations with their peers and teachers.[56] They are calmer, happier and more

56. See, for example, Jonathan Campion & Sharn Rocco (2009) *Minding the Mind: The Effects and Potential of a School-Based Meditation Programme for Mental Health Promotion*, in *Advances in School Mental Health Promotion*, Vol 2:1 ; also the separate but similar organisations: *'Meditation in Schools'*, and *'Mindfulness in Schools'*. See Appendix 2 for their website details.

mature, learning about the value of co-operation as well as that of competition; learning to respect their rivals, becoming increasingly appreciative of the opportunities that different opponents present them for self-development.

Many schoolteachers make an effort to retain, express and share regularly their own sense of wonder concerning the subjects they teach, rather than reduce them to text book summaries and the dull repetition of 'facts' for later regurgitation by pupils in their examinations. This is necessary and appropriate when aiming to foster, rather than inhibit, the inherent spiritual tendency of children to greet nature and respond to it with energetic curiosity, awe, amazement, delight and a genuine sense of mystery. It seems especially necessary, in the pursuit of wisdom on behalf of each child, for science teachers to ensure that science and spirituality are presented as being in true harmony with one another.

* * *

12

HEALTH, MENTAL HEALTH AND SOCIAL CARE

Compared with the Victorian era, health and social services in western democracies have improved enormously. Screening and other sickness prevention programmes, for example, demonstrate a high degree of social maturity. At a worldly level, they reveal financial acumen, warding off the risk of greater subsequent costs by discovering and treating problems at an early stage, allowing people to feel more secure in regard to their health as they advance through life. On the other hand, it is more difficult to assess whether much progress has been made at the spiritual level; to what degree kindness and compassion hold sway, or how much reliance on the scientific approach and the 'medical model' may have had a possibly negative, dehumanising effect on patients and staff alike.

Matters are even more difficult to clarify when, for example, a person's liberty is removed (albeit temporarily) under Mental Health legislation if, through mental illness, they are at risk of self-harm or behaving in a dangerous manner. It is clearly in the best interests of the community for such a person to be 'sectioned' and removed, but it is only in that person's best interest if they then receive high quality assessment, treatment and care in a safe, nurturing environment, attended by skilled staff, and released again into a suitably supportive environment, not prematurely, but when their mental health has been as fully restored as possible.

It is costly to provide this level of mental health care, and it requires much more than financial expenditure. It requires suitable buildings, which may be affordable, but also large numbers of highly trained mental health professionals: doctors, nurses, social workers, psychologists, occupational therapists, pharmacists, administrators and others. Furthermore, this is not only about financial expense; it is also about self-sacrifice. All of these people commit themselves to years of training. Typically on relatively modest incomes meanwhile, they usually incur a degree of personal debt, but only one aspect of their sacrifice concerns money. They will face high levels of hard to remedy human suffering on a more or less daily basis.

From the worldly perspective, the training received, together with regular subsequent financial remuneration and the promise of a healthy pension, provide considerable incentives; but these benefits are easily undermined within a hierarchical organisation governed by financial and political targets, where the good of the organisation apparently (despite worthy 'mission statements') takes precedence over the welfare of the individual, whether staff member, patient or members of a patient's family. The situation worsens further when recruitment problems add to the burden of workload, which threatens quickly to become excessive and worsens again whenever pay fails to keep pace with inflation, making the job less attractive, and making recruitment even harder.

Whether anxious, depressed, demented, deluded, hallucinating or 'acting out' in a destructive or self-destructive manner, people experiencing mental illness are challenging to look after. This invokes another dimension of self-sacrifice: deep personal commitment to the well-being of patients. This is a challenge because, without wisdom and compassion, it is easy to fall prey to fatigue, frustration, cruelty and despair.

It is difficult, in other words, to maintain the required levels of energy, courage, kindness and hope. Compassion, 'suffering with' others in their distress, needs tempering with the wisdom that recognises the need for adequate time for recovery and revival, for rest and re-creation. The care-giver's first priority is therefore, paradoxically, to care properly for oneself. A vital aspect of this, particularly for the more spiritually mature and insightful, is likely to involve engaging in regular forms of spiritual practice, to ensure regular top-ups of spiritual energy and continuing progress along the pathway to wisdom.

Much the same applies to those working with people, especially children and young people, who have physical health problems; for example those facing disfigurement, suffering permanent or recurrent pain, or some form of disability. It applies equally when treating people in great distress and anguish, perhaps as a result of medical or surgical interventions or through being terminally ill. However difficult and emotionally painful this work is at times, though, when faced with a mature and enduring combination of acceptance, calm, faith and hope, many find it extremely worthwhile.

It sometimes happens that, at an early age, a person 'knows' that they are destined to become, for example, a doctor or nurse. This is 'vocation', a spiritual experience involving a sense of being called to do something selfless, great and useful to others. Implicit in accepting such a calling is the faith that one has the predisposing character, intelligence and aptitude for the training and the challenges to follow, and that somehow, whenever needed, through a kind of 'grace', motivation, energy, guidance and strength will be found within, vouchsafed as a gift or blessing by the great, holy, spirit-breath-energy of the universe. The inner determination to succeed in gaining the required qualifications, and to master the required skills, depends on one's essentially spiritual conviction that all is as it is meant to be, whether through 'fate', 'destiny', 'karma', 'kismet', 'Providence' perhaps, or 'God's will'; and that nothing can or will stand in one's way. When barriers arise, they too are seen as part of the process, to be overcome with persistence or circumvented with wisdom.

Such a journey is, in a sense, its own reward. Regular remuneration and later a pension are pleasing but not central considerations. Even success with patients is a secondary feature; partly through humility, taking account of knowing that nature heals and health professionals only assist in the natural process; also because one counter-balancing failure can offset many successes.

Day by day, year by year, the most satisfying reward for commitment to helping others is a sense of growth, of becoming increasingly true to one's higher nature, to one's 'spiritual self', giving in less readily to the worldly temptations of a pleasure-seeking life and the lures of luxury, wealth, power and fame. From the first day at medical or nursing school, the health care student is faced with the facts of human suffering, of all manner of pain: physical, psychological, social and spiritual. In western culture, the emphasis is on scientific knowledge, on related diagnostic and other technology, and on pharmaceuticals and surgery to assess, correct and cure symptoms, to suppress physical and emotional pain. Progress along these lines has been phenomenal and is to be applauded. Curing symptoms, however, is not the same as healing people. To heal, in this context, means 'to make whole', and this is essentially spiritual work, requiring a different, complementary approach alongside the basic fixing of problems.

Students are largely discouraged from thinking and enquiring about patients whose condition, whether medical, surgical or psychiatric, cannot be cured or much improved. They are asked to trust and accept blindly that science will one day find the necessary solution. Worldly values prevail, and specialties that promise speedy and effective treatments (surgery, in particular) are considered more praiseworthy, are more popular, and are better remunerated than those dealing with more intractable problems, for example dermatology, rheumatology, neurology and psychiatry. The wisdom approach, however, would be to re-balance this situation, aware that equally valuable but different skills and personal characteristics are required in the different situations.

Even from a worldly viewpoint, helping to keep a young person with schizophrenia functioning in society, with his or her symptoms under reasonable control for most of a lifetime, is arguably of at least as much value to the community as the surgical repair of an injury that enables an adult to return to the work-force. From the spiritual perspective, though, there is the additional benefit *to the practitioner* of engaging fully with the same patients over a period. This is a situation which used to be common in general practice when whole families, generation by generation, were signed up with and treated by a single GP, but it is no longer the usual case. The opportunities for personal growth are more abundant when such a situation prevails than during the brief, often relatively impersonal, encounters between today's health care professionals and their patients.

Such matters are seldom put up for discussion before medical or nursing students, who may develop their own preferences and inclinations; but this is a missed opportunity. Third-year medical students who attended for teaching about spirituality and health care reported, for example, the following:

- Although the 'holistic' or 'biopsychosocial' approach to healthcare dominated the rhetoric of the teaching they received, spirituality was not usually mentioned.

- Previously equating spirituality exclusively with religion, after the course students recognised a clear distinction between the two,

- Also that a person's spirituality is not dependent on religious affiliation, conviction or practice.

- Hesitant to discuss spirituality with their teachers and colleagues before the course, students much preferred afterwards being open, feeling adequately equipped now to discuss the subject.

- Before, neither religion nor spirituality were considered by students to have a place in modern, scientific, evidence-based medicine. Afterwards, they considered patients' spirituality important, recommending that it be assessed routinely. They said that all healthcare staff should be able to 'take a spiritual history'[57], as they had learned to do, so that appropriate steps could be initiated to meet patients' spiritual needs where possible.

- Students reported that taking a spiritual history alone seemed to benefit some patients. One reported, for example, *'I have been a medical student for three years and that's the first time I have come away feeling I've actually helped somebody.'* [58]

By the end of the short course, the self-selected students were also able to demonstrate a satisfactory general overview of spiritual and religious factors that might affect health and the course of an illness. The idea that people continue to grow spiritually throughout life, especially through adversity, resonated positively with several course attenders. Some reported regretting previously neglecting their own spiritual development. Some, who had been having doubts

57. See Larry Culliford (2007) Taking a Spiritual History, *Advances in Psychiatric Treatment*, 13:3.

58. See Larry Culliford (2009) Teaching Spirituality and Health Care to Third Year Medical Students, *The Clinical Teacher*, 6:1.

about its relevance to their careers in medicine, expressed their gratitude and relief, saying the course had rekindled their optimism by giving the spiritual dimension renewed importance in following their chosen career.

Such observations show how widely, almost universally, the secular, materialistic, left-brain approach has been adopted in the field of health care, but also how quickly such perceptive students can firstly recognise the incompleteness of the teaching, then make up the deficit. The spiritual approach is not contrary to the more typical, binary, sick/well medical model of health care. It is complementary, enhancing it and is therefore of particularly special value whenever the limits of traditional medicine and surgery have been reached, when anyone is facing disfigurement, disability, dementia, for example, or death.

According to Monika Renz, a psychotherapist and spiritual caregiver, who works with dying patients as head of the psycho-oncology department of a large hospital in St Gallen, Switzerland:

Dying persons undergo a transition, which consists essentially of a transformation of perception. As we approach death, all egoism and ego-centred perception (what I wanted, thought, felt), and all ego-based needs fade into the background. Coming to the fore is another world, state of consciousness, sensitivity, and thus another way of experiencing being, relationship, connectedness, and dignity. All this occurs irrespective of the individual's worldview and faith.[59]

59. Monika Renz (2015) *Dying: a transition,* New York: Columbia University Press.p 17. See also Monika Renz (2016) *Hope and Grace: spiritual experiences in severe distress, illness and dying,* Jessica Kingsley Publishers.

This final phase of life continues to hold great potential, and to be of significant value, as spiritual growth continues right until people take their final breath. Renz's observations are backed by the research of psychologists Reza Arasteh and Steve Taylor,[60] who both found similar changes indicating marked shifts forward in terms of spiritual development in people facing or following extreme ego-threatening situations including terminal illness.

Hospices, as well as hospitals, can therefore be considered valuable places to work, volunteer or simply visit, acting as informal 'spiritual universities', treasure houses of spiritual experience. That they are the focus of, and owe their continuing existence to, an immense amount of charity work, adds to their value within communities. Some hospices have recognised the broader context of their work and provide outreach facilities, including some hosting a 'schools project'.[61] This offers a short, structured series of visits for groups of about a dozen ten-to-twelve-year-old children with their teachers, who meet and engage with patients, family members and staff, volunteers and perhaps also recently bereaved people in a safe, supportive and fully supervised environment that is said, perhaps surprisingly, to promise 'lots of fun and laughter'. Such projects, in addressing myths and reducing anxiety around loss and bereavement, help create in children, and their parents (who are invited to attend one of the sessions), healthier attitudes towards death, dying and life transition. Like other related outreach projects, schools projects also build links and raise awareness in the community about the hospice's work and purpose.

The conveners of one such hospice-based schools project describe a heart-warming honesty, directness and openness among their young visitors; a typical comment being, *'They*

60. See A Reza Arasteh (1975).

61. For example, the St Barnabas Hospice 'schools project'. See Appendix 2 for website details.

handle the situation here better than many grown-ups'. This clearly supports observations about children's innate spiritual awareness reported in the preceding chapter. Children can be teachers too.

* * *

13

CAPITALISM – ECONOMICS, BANKING AND BUSINESS

The apparent clash between worldly and spiritual values that features in the context of health and social care is even more marked in regard to economics, banking and business. Capitalism, an integral and largely beneficial aspect of western democracy, involves private wealth being used to provide services, also to produce and sell goods, for financial profit. The system is enabled by the stock market, and by banks offering loans and mortgages, also in the interests of financial gain. The necessary promotion of consumerism accounts for the universal use of advertising and other forms of commercial inducement, which lead directly to a widespread general preoccupation with such goods and services. While the 'spiritual self' remains unmoved, such a system is mightily appealing to the 'everyday ego'. Capitalism thus implicitly promotes immature, left-brain induced, worldly values to those who are susceptible. As such, it risks a proliferation of desire, greed, excess and wastage on one hand, scarcity, debt, poverty and inequality on the other.

People up to 'Conformist' Stage 3, in seeking to belong, do not want to miss out or feel left behind by their peer group. They essentially want to keep up, for example by having many 'followers' and being much 'liked' on social media. They also have a strong tendency to *worry*: about what other people think of them, about their appearance, their social status, their wealth (or lack of it), and much more. It is a fallacy, fed by commerce and advertising, that freedom from worry and lasting contentment come when a person has whatever they want in terms of wealth, position and an associated abundance of everyday goods and services. The need to defend one's position and protect one's possessions is energy-sapping. Envy and resentment are rife. Excess often results in satiety and boredom, triggering a near-perpetual search for novelty and stimulation. The success of commercial advertising depends upon this. Adverts are specifically designed, *'To create an anxiety relieved by a purchase'*, as one consumerist authority has said. This notion sadly underpins the unkindest of fallacies on which the capitalist system is based.

Internet companies have also learned to target individuals with personalised advertising based on computer analysis of their 'likes' and other preferences. Goods and services are presented ever more seductively as so-called *'click-bait'*; and a particularly unwise form of advertising preys on whatever residual spiritual awareness exists within a person, corrupting the fragile flame of maturity through the use of spiritual and religious ideas and images ('icons'), to promote luxury goods: chocolates, perfumes, holidays and fast cars, for example, none of which are either necessary or spiritually beneficial.

In order to keep up with the temptations spread before them, people become convinced they 'need' things, rather than simply 'desire' them. To be able to buy the desired goods and services, a preoccupation with personal income and job security becomes an overriding concern. This level of disquiet is heightened for those who are poor, also for those with debts and mortgages. This anxiety, in turn, sets the scene for rivalry between people seeking limited work opportunities, resulting in intolerance and sometimes strong antipathy towards, for example, strangers and immigrants, characterised unfairly as undeserving interlopers. All this contributes to the multiple inter-penetrating vicious circles of human suffering outlined in Chapter 1.

Rifts arise too between employees and their employers, whose jobs and (usually much higher) incomes depend in turn on maintaining commercial profitability. Work, rather than being a creative and fulfilling aspect of an individual's daily life, part of a rewarding spiritual journey, risks becoming only a means to an end, the simple goal of livelihood at the personal and family level, the means to pay for both necessary and superfluous-but-desirable goods and services. The goals at the level of the employing organisation and the wider political state include principally commercial success and 'wealth creation' to provide perpetual economic growth.

On the positive side, there are countless ways in which capitalism has brought benefits to individuals and society, not least through free or subsidised housing, education and health care, also military and police protection, fire and sea rescue services, public transport and many other civic amenities, such as effective sewerage and waste disposal. It is also very encouraging to be aware of the extraordinary beneficence of wealthy philanthropists, and the immense amount of beneficial work of many types conducted by many well-supported charities. These too can be seen as integral to the capitalist way of life. It could be unpopular, therefore, to indicate and dwell on the flaws inherent in such a money-and-goods obsessed system. In the interests of wisdom and maturity, though, it must be admitted that there are destructive consequences to consumerism. A significant number of inter-related ills can be seen to affect society as a direct or indirect effect of the imperatives inherent in such an apparently relentless profit-motivated attitude whenever spiritual values are subordinated to worldly ones.

To begin with, precious minerals, plants and forests, fossil fuels and other natural resources are required in abundance to feed western economies, and large amounts of inert or noxious waste products must be disposed of or recycled. The tendency is for resource-poor countries and territories to be neglected, and resource-rich lands to be plundered by those states and organisations already rich and powerful. Negative consequences include the possibility of political upheaval and armed conflict, also the grave threat of ecological damage.

Goods and services provided by political states, often in combination with private enterprise, include the weapons and delivery systems of war, so-called 'defence', and other forms of aggression, together with multiple back-up services. These reap enormous and relied-upon contributions to the economy, risking a heedless hunt for financial gain that may easily override other important considerations, and severely compromise spiritual values and the universal search for wisdom.

It seems worth repeating that armed aggression regularly results in large numbers of destitute and dependent refugees. Other consequences of capitalist economics and the huge international corporations of 'big business' also include global warming, climate change and unstable weather patterns, leading to an increase in natural catastrophes like hurricanes, floods, famine, forest fires and coastal destruction due to melting polar ice and rising sea levels, with a further resulting increase in the numbers of disaster victims and refugees.

Closer to home, people in the earlier stages of spiritual development, in the absence of meaningful and satisfying employment, are at risk of suffering a kind of spiritual 'malaise', falling prey to symptoms like anxiety and depression, reducing further their likelihood of finding and holding onto a job. Comfort eating may lead to obesity. Smoking causes heart disease and cancer; and a range of other destructive addictions lie in wait for those who seek distraction from tedium, people concerned not with spiritual comfort and personal development, but with ultimately futile attempts either to numb or avoid physical and emotional pain and suffering.

Addictions are extreme forms of attachment, and frequently indicate a degree of spiritual immaturity and distress.

While some addictions are less harmful than others (running, for example, dancing, or playing bridge), others are exceptionally destructive, hurting not only those affected, but also their friends and family, and the wider community. The most harmful and costly for society include addictions to sex, gambling, nicotine, alcohol, prescription medications and other drugs like heroin and cocaine. These, in turn, give rise to another level of social destruction through crime, particularly 'organised crime', which preys especially on vulnerable people. Such crime includes people trafficking, modern slavery, forced prostitution, drug production, smuggling and selling, money laundering, and tax evasion. Often, these go together.

Policing these matters is difficult and expensive. Offenders, when caught, require and deserve punishment, but also understanding and skilled rehabilitation. This, too, to reduce re-offending, is in society's best interest. Investment in addicts and offenders when young, especially at school age, seems likely to yield the most beneficial results, so it is discouraging to read of significant school drop-out rates, a rise in gang conflict, acid attacks, gun and knife crime among teenagers, the 'county lines' drug distribution system, and an official description of child offender units as 'unsafe'. One hopeful prediction, however, is that, with advancing spiritual maturity among the population at large, generation by generation, such tragic problems and the associated suffering are quite capable of gradually fading away.

* * *

Light and dark balance each other. The wisdom approach is to see all the social ills and benefits of capitalism as seamlessly inter-related. For the present and immediate future, it is necessary to accept that one aspect goes with the other, like yin and yang, night and day. For improvement to occur, it has become a question of restoring a balance between worldly and spiritual values.

A quote from the Indian promoter of non-violence, Mahatma Gandhi, *'Be the change that you want to see in the world'*,[62] serves to remind us that, rather than government-led social engineering, the best way forward involves individuals committing themselves to making progress, and helping others make similar progress, towards wisdom and maturity. Many people carry out some form of a Spiritual Development Plan (SDP) or a Personal Growth Programme (PGP). They may do so either automatically and unconsciously or deliberately and consciously; the latter thus starting out purposefully on the journey of the second half of their lives, exploring profitably the spiritual dimension of human understanding and experience. Part 3 looks more closely into that highly recommended pathway.

* * *

62. See Appendix 2 for website details about Gandhi quotes.

14

ART AND CREATIVITY

Art can be said to form a living bridge between mind and spirit, between the psychological and spiritual dimensions of human experience. This is the primary reason artists create, and why others value their art.

A clear distinction must be made between art and merchandise. True art, according to the wisdom view, avoids materialist contamination, and reflects spiritual principles and values like beauty and creativity. It therefore depends on the honesty, generosity, discernment, patience and perseverance of the artist. To situate art in the market-place can easily result in spiritually impoverished ephemera, the production of which is governed by worldly priorities like profit, success, power, status and fame.

Spiritual writer Thomas Merton (whose parents were both artists, and who was himself a notable poet, calligrapher and photographer) wrote in a letter to Boris Pasternak in October 1958, *'I do not insist on this division between spirituality and art, for I think that even things that are not patently spiritual if they come from the heart of a spiritual person are spiritual'*.[63]

63. Thomas Merton (2008) *Thomas Merton: A LIfe in Letters – the essential collection*, selected and edited by William Shannon and Christine Bochen. New York: Harper Collins, p 109.

If art comes from the heart and, likewise, speaks to the heart, this asks something of the witness too. It requires a kind of emotional and spiritual sensitivity with which to receive the generous gift of the artist, whether painter, sculptor, musician, photographer, calligrapher or in other ways grace-filled and talented.

Here is another brief personal anecdote, one connecting art and spirituality. I remember, some years ago, standing transfixed before a self-portrait of an older Rembrandt in an exhibition in London. It was hot and crowded in that dark, airless space. I was aware of people coming and going beside me, but remained standing there in a kind of timeless personal bubble, filled with fascination and wonder. I also recall a similar experience when, as a teenager on a family holiday in Spain, I heard on the radio for the first time Rodrigo's magnificent piece for guitar and orchestra, the *Concerto de Aranjuez*. Entranced, delighted and awestruck for its entire duration, I did not want it to end. These were not simply aesthetic experiences, moments of pleasure. They were, I would say, spiritual experiences, because they were in some small way transformative. I was not entirely the same person afterwards but somehow indefinably wiser and better connected, through the art and the artist, to my fellow human beings and to the cosmic whole. I consider it proof of this that the most vivid and delightful memory of these experiences has stayed with me ever since.

How may engaging with the arts and performing acts of creativity help in developing wisdom? The 'spiritual practices' discussed in Part Three, designed to further one's journey on the path of spiritual growth and development, include: *'Appreciation of the arts and engaging in creative activities'*, also, *'Reading poetry and literature'*. As far as this goes, consistent with ideas presented in Chapter 5, the left hemisphere of the brain is required to read the words, and the right hemisphere is needed to provide context and imagery. People who read music or lyrics, which they then play or sing, are similarly powerfully harmonising the left and right brains. A third form of spiritual practice listed is therefore, *'Engaging with music'*, which includes listening, chanting and dancing, as well as playing and singing.

Specifically sacred music might be involved here, but not necessarily. Many forms and styles of music are capable of releasing something profoundly emotional – some sadness, perhaps, or great joy – that has been imprisoned hitherto by excessive attention to worldly concerns and the busy pursuit of secular activities. Rhythmical and repetitive dance (like that of Sufism's whirling dervishes) and chanting (whether Gregorian chant, or the kirtan and bhajans of the sacred Hindu and Jain traditions), bringing left and right brain together, as similarly happens during meditation, form a powerful bridge between a particular form of art and a deeply personal spiritual experience. Furthermore, people coming together to engage in such practices, as when playing in an orchestra or singing in a choir, may well experience enhancement, through sharing, in terms of spiritual gain.

Art and human creativity provide further evidence that everyone is spiritually connected to everyone else. *'We are already one'*, as Thomas Merton once wrote, *'But we imagine that we are not. And what we have to recover is our original unity... What we have to be is what we are'*.[64] Art can help us do that.

* * *

---

64. Thomas Merton (1973) *The Asian Journal of Thomas Merton,* p 308.

PART THREE
Seeking Wisdom

Things You May Want To Do

'We must learn to live together as sisters and brothers, or we will perish together as fools.'[65]

No one is too small to make a difference. [66]

65. Martin Luther King Jr. quoted by Archbishop Desmond Tutu in Dalai Lama & Desmond Tutu, with Douglas Abrams (2016) *The Book of Joy: lasting happiness in a changing world*. London: Hutchinson.p 270.

66. Greta Thunberg (2019) *No One Is Too Small To Make A Difference*. London: Penguin/Random House, p 14.

15

TOWARDS MATURITY

Wisdom, based on the idea of seamless universal connectedness, strongly suggests that the way forward for global culture in the overlapping spheres of politics, religion, education, health and social care, economics and art cannot realistically be prescribed as a joint enterprise, *en masse*, unless engaged in willingly by individuals at a deeply personal level.

Faced with an extensive diet of human suffering, transmitted twenty-four hours daily through the media, a person's first natural impulses are 'to do something' and to call on others to do something, to petition people in positions of authority and power. At home, for example, we want the police to solve crimes and keep us safe. Elsewhere, we similarly want the Prime Minister, the President, and the United Nations to force a stop to the bombing of innocent people. We acknowledge that much is done, and done charitably, when both natural and man-made disasters occur, but onlookers necessarily remain aware of much untouched and irresolvable anguish and misery in the aftermath. Not every catastrophe can be prevented in the first place or put right afterwards.

This leaves many of us in the role of near-helpless bystanders, at risk of despair, in a negative frame of mind that involves powerful feelings of dissatisfaction, anger, guilt and shame. If asked, 'Where is the pain?' many will point to the tragedy on the television screen and say, *'Out there... Look!'* Wisdom suggests, though, that it may be better for people to remain reflective, recognising that the only pain we can take full responsibility for and deal with directly lies within our own hearts and minds.

Remember the story from Chapter 7 in which the teacher asked, 'Where is the pain, Larry?' In doing so, he helped me recognise that compassion is part of human nature, and that (as the Latin words from which it takes its meaning indicate) it involves suffering... 'suffering with' other people. Problems arise particularly when that essential human response is rejected. 'Feeling bad is not the problem, Larry', the kindly monk told me. 'Feeling bad *about* feeling bad: that's essentially the problem'.

An important aspect of the way forward, in other words, is to permit feelings of grief to surface; to identify with the suffering of others and lament. This is one of the first and most valuable lessons when seeking wisdom and maturity. Lamentation is not the same as being depressed. The grieving process is purposeful. As described in Chapter 4, it flows naturally in the direction of healing and growth. Containing vital seeds of recovery, it represents a valuable source of hope.

Of course, it is not easy to embrace pain, and the present cultural norm is to reject this option. Nevertheless, to make progress towards wisdom and maturity, to grow as a person, it is necessary to become aware of the painful emotions that arise in the face of loss; to feel okay about them, if possible, without adding an extra layer by feeling bad about them. Trying to ignore or dismiss them does no lasting good. Instead, it is necessary to cultivate an attitude of acceptance, to allow the full interplay of feelings into consciousness, including sadness and the accompanying release of tears, so that nature's healing solution can begin working towards fruition.

Maturity also means restraining oneself from speaking out or acting in response to any destructive or self-destructive impulses that might be provoked through painful emotions, notably those of fear, anger or guilt; so it becomes a matter for individuals to develop an ever-increasing level of emotional stability over time; and there are many ways to achieve this.

When the pain is close to home – a person's own suffering, or that of a beloved family member, for example – a shift in perspective, from anguish and misery to wisdom and compassion, will depend in part on recognising and feeling genuinely, with a true heart, that others elsewhere are suffering too. Such a change brings the comforting knowledge that one is not alone, prompting the healing idea that all human suffering may be shared.

It is not enough, then, for people simply to conform within society. It is not even enough to seek independence, taking some measure of individual responsibility for one's intentions, words and actions. It is necessary to go further along life's journey, experiencing oneself as seamlessly connected to the whole, to everyone else, to nature and the fullness of creation.

Making progress on the spiritual path into the second half of life, going past 'Conformist' Stage 3 and 'Individual' Stage 4, beyond self-centred egocentricity towards selfless universality, comes about in one sense through the letting go of both attachments and aversions. This is more difficult and painful in the earlier stages, when we people hold on tightly to what we have and what we believe. A key insight, though, is that, with growing maturity, relinquishing a degree of attachment does not necessarily involve losing the object of attachment itself. This subtle distinction makes things easier, allowing us to continue the enjoyment of specific objects, places, activities, ideas, and even relations with other people, without being as rigid, dependent and possessive about them as before. Love between people, for example, is purified in this way, becoming less demanding and more generous. Maturity delivers rewards because, in giving up attachments and, particularly, aversions, the process becomes increasingly liberating. The process of letting go is accompanied more frequently by feelings of relief, satisfaction, joy and laughter, which take the place of grieving, sorrow and tears.

With maturity, particularly from 'Integration' Stage 5 onwards, a kind of 'homecoming' begins. The tension between one's false 'everyday ego' and true 'spiritual self' diminishes. It is usually a gradual process, but sometimes occurs following a breakthrough spiritual experience, some kind of epiphany during which 'something happens', something inexplicable, beyond words. Such a breakthrough is hard to predict and plan for, but progress – gradual or sudden – is more likely when you adopt a formal or informal wisdom-seeking Personal Growth Programme (PGP) or Spiritual Development Plan (SDP), consisting of regularly engaging in holistic or spiritual practices.

* * *

Wisdom practices of a holistic and spiritual nature can be divided into two main types: religious and secular. These are of time-honoured value, and have in common that they improve personal harmony by restoring an ideal balance between the left and right brain hemispheres, and thus between spiritual and worldly values. These practices promote personal equanimity in the face of threats and also foster natural grieving and healing in the face of loss, with personal growth as a natural and permanent consequence. Between people, even people from widely different backgrounds who may not even have a common language, shared holistic and spiritual practices tend to promote fellow-feeling and friendship.

The simplest daily wisdom practice routine, PGP or SDP, might consist of five parts:

a) Regular quiet time (for meditation, reflection or prayer);

b) Appropriate study (of religious, spiritual or other wisdom material);

c) Maintaining supportive friendships with others who share similar humanitarian or spiritual aims and values;

d) Regular acts of kindness and compassion

e)Time spent engaging with nature.

The value of stillness and silence, often coupled with solitude, is paramount in the service of wisdom. *'Simply being with yourself'* is the essence of the practice of meditation, which involves focused concentration on a stable, unobtrusive stimulus – such as one's own breath flowing back and forth; a static image; or a simple sound, like a brief phrase or prayer.

Importantly, one's mind is allowed to settle, so that internal as well as external stimulation softens and the mind begins to focus upon itself – to notice without disturbance the thoughts, emotions, sense perceptions and impulses that arise. Eventually, with practice, even residual mental content subsides, leaving the mind entirely clear and alert.

This 'mindful' mental state, devoid of the 'everyday ego', is expansive and full of energy. It can seem endless or bottomless, yet there is no partitioning within it, and no room for anything else. This is the essence of unitary, 'holistic', 'mindful' experience, the natural state of the 'spiritual self', fully in tune with itself and in tune with the universe.

The benefits are cumulative, as practitioners persist and skill is acquired, and they extend well outside the meditation sessions. Neuroscience research has shown that even short periods of regular mindfulness practice, silent prayer or 'stilling', can reshape the brain's neural pathways, increasing those areas associated with kindness, compassion and rationality, while decreasing those involved with anxiety, worry and impulsiveness.

Meditation involves more than simply employing various techniques. It is a mysterious process that occurs spontaneously as a gap opens up when the mind becomes engaged purely with itself, a time during which it is more likely that 'something happens' to promote spiritual growth than during everyday waking consciousness. The only way to assess the benefits of meditation, and to achieve its precious fruit, is to engage in and persevere with the practice personally, to undertake it rigorously like any scientific experiment. To try out meditation therefore involves acting in faith. Not quite identical to religious faith, this is faith in some aspect of nature that can confidently be predicted, like the healing of a flesh wound, or the changing sequence of the seasons.

Meditation forms a key component of the mystical paths of most world religions, but it is a discipline that is increasingly engaged in too by those who count themselves atheist or 'spiritual but not religious'. Both religious and non-religious people presumably experience similar promptings from their inner compass or guide, impulses for self-improvement arising from an uncomfortable tension between the worldly, false 'everyday ego' and the more transcendent, authentic 'spiritual self'. To cater for this, a number of other religious and spiritual practices also have secular counterparts, as in the following lists.

Religious practices, in addition to meditation and prayer, include:

a) Worship and other forms of ritual practices;
b) Reading scripture and studying theology;
c) Listening to, singing and playing sacred music;
d) Undertaking spiritual retreats;
e) Going on pilgrimages to sacred sites; and
f) Through service, doing vocational and charitable work.

Their secular equivalents include:

g) Folk traditions and rituals;
h) Contemplative reading of poetry, philosophy, fine literature and good quality self-help advice;

i) Engaging with uplifting or 'soulful' music –
through listening, singing, chanting, playing and
dancing; and
j) Through regular acts of kindness and compassion.

Whether religious or not, people utilise additional similar
methods of spiritual refreshment and renewal, often combining
several, for example:

k) Maintaining stable and loving family relationships
and friendships;
l) Engaging with and enjoying nature – connecting
in various ways with the sea and the countryside,
spending time outdoors in the air, in wilderness
places, conservation reserves, parklands and gardens;
m) Physical activity and keeping healthy; and
n) Appreciation of the arts and engaging in creative
activities.

Just as people come together in churches, synagogues,
mosques, temples and Sikh gurdwaras, not only to cement their
faith and worship but also to engage in community activities
and communal life, so do secular groupings arise to engage in
co-operative activities of a sporting, educational, recreational
or charitable nature, or other types of group work and play, in
ways that involve a special quality of non-partisan bonding and
friendship. When spiritual values are adopted and adhered to
like this, harm is avoided and great benefit possible.

With increasing spiritual maturity, both religious devotion
and civic duty feel less like burdensome servitude, more like
joyful liberation. Until these rewards are felt, though, as may
often be the case with the newly committed, a temptation
could grow to abandon the intention to adopt regular wisdom
practices. Seeking the company and support of others on
the path to wisdom and spiritual maturity helps offset this.
Reading encouraging stories about spiritual masters, teachers,

saintly, virtue-filled heroes and heroines who have persevered in the face of great challenges, offers another way forward when discouragement threatens. [67]

It must be admitted, however, that not everyone is prepared to go forward. Some struggle with and actively resist, for various reasons, the arguments in favour of, and the opportunities to benefit from, wisdom-seeking behaviour. The tyrannical left-brain, intolerant of change, insisting it knows best, holds many in its powerful gravitational pull. Its victims can be seen to suffer as a result, and it is natural for those a little further along the path to maturity to want to help and encourage them. We are understandably loath to turn away from them in their ignorance and apparently avoidable anguish, but caution is required. It can be necessary to protect oneself if those you try to assist behave in a threatening or destructive manner. Even then, as long as it is not totally overwhelming, one may be able to make use of their opposition and hostility by learning from it. Worth bearing constantly in mind, however, is the most important priority: your own spiritual progress. Keep that in focus, and everything else will then flow.

* * *

---

67. A remarkably courageous but little known 20th century example is Etty Hillesum, who died in Auschwitz in 1943. See Larry Culliford (2011) *The Psychology of Spirituality: an introduction*, London: Jessica Kingsley Publishers, pp 180-190.

16

ADOPTING A PLAN

Eventually, when someone decides that making progress towards wisdom and spiritual maturity has become their priority for life, we can ask, 'What does this entail?'

Even before reaching that point, it can be a good idea to evaluate oneself, and to do so in a generous and forgiving, optimistic way. This will involve taking time to think about life in the long-term, about your priorities and values, and so assess your current position on the pathway towards further growth. To what extent, for example, are you a conformer with others, comfortable in a group, knowing you belong to the majority or at least a strong minority? To what degree, on the other hand, do you prefer to think, speak and act independently? If independent, what is your agenda? What, and who, do you put first in life?

There are no correct or incorrect answers to these questions. They are simply pointers to help people get an indication about progress already made, and the tasks that still lie ahead. This is a private matter, not a public examination or competition.

In addressing these questions, it helps to recall that there are different life priorities at the different stages of spiritual development. In 'Conformist' Stage 3, which all go through, we form attachments based on what we like, and aversions based on what we dislike, largely in the interests of both personal gratification and social integration. We do this through acquiring prized allegiances, status and possessions, and by denying or rejecting whatever seems uncomfortable, alien and contradictory.

In 'Individual' Stage 4, our priorities shift naturally towards self-discovery, developing oneself as an independent and responsible *observer* as well as *participant* in one's own life. It usually means relinquishing some former attachments and adjusting to the resulting uncertainty and relative isolation.

In making a self-assessment and working towards progress on the wisdom path, it is best to seek help, advice and encouragement from those already wise and mature, but spiritual guides are not widespread or easily identifiable in western culture; also, caution: false guides (often unashamedly self-promoting) can present a significant problem, leading people astray. It is therefore unfortunately the case for many that it becomes necessary to discover reliable methods, implement a plan, and forge ahead for oneself. It is often necessary to overcome the strong influence of rigid left-brain thought processes, which tend to reject anything new, even in the face of good evidence. Once inner resistance is overcome and the decision to seek wisdom is made, however, spiritual backing and support can be relied on eventually, through synchronicity, to appear. As a wisdom saying has it, 'Wherever there is a pupil, there will be a teacher'.

In making any self-evaluation, it is wise to be scrupulously honest and avoid false modesty. The most helpful question to keep asking is, simply, '*Who am I?*' until a new understanding of oneself as a universal being, at one with others, nature and the sacred cosmic whole, is achieved. Initially, of course, the obvious answer to 'Who am I?' is simply, '*I am a person, a human being*', followed by basic personal details: names, place of birth, where you live, nationality, race, primary language (including accent or dialect), sexual orientation and preferences, social class, religious (or non-religious) affiliation, and/or political persuasion.

We also identify ourselves as family members (parent, sibling, child, aunt, uncle and so on) and according to marital status. Other relevant details include levels of education, income and wealth, health/illness ability/disability status, type of work, preferred style of dress, diet, hobbies, preferences for music and media viewing, sports interests and other matters.

All of this more or less pins us down as a person, the kind of information that helps others know *about* us, but not necessarily to *know* us as 'who we really are', to encounter our essence and feel any kind of loving, caring, devotional bond. Other questions are needed to draw us closer to people, questions like, *'What else motivates you at the deepest level?'* and *'Where do you draw strength, hope and courage from, when you face challenges… when times are really hard*?' These are more spiritual types of question that are well worth asking ourselves from time to time.

In both Stages 3 and 4, wisdom practices forming a Personal Growth Programme (PGP) or Spiritual Development Plan (SDP) can be relied on to promote progress towards the next stage and onward. Part of the recommended self-evaluation process therefore includes going carefully through the list of exercises in Chapter 15, taking a kind of spiritual inventory to identify those with which you are already engaging, and those which you might be inclined to add to your routine.

Many people already take care of their spiritual needs and hunger automatically, through natural and spontaneous impulses, topping up regularly on vital spiritual energy in various ways, imbibing as it were from the great sacred unity of creation, from the great cosmic wind or holy spirit, both alone and in supportive groups. It does no harm to connect increasingly consciously, perhaps coming to recognise that your daily walk with the dog, time spent in the garden, regular act of kindness for a neighbour, work in a charity shop, volunteering in a school, hospital or hospice, your weekly music lesson, art class, game of bridge or football and so on, any and all of which, or a host of similar practices, may be a key contributing factor, not only in regard to psychological well-being but also in boosting your personal growth towards spiritual maturity.

It does no harm, either, to think of new ways of enriching one's life. Here is spiritual coach Heather Jane-James on the subject:

> *I have never been anywhere in the world that there wasn't something to wonder at. Ever... Start looking. Every day for a month make a conscious decision to stop and stare at something small like a flower, change your planned journeys to include a scenic route and stop and get out, take pictures. So many of us have decent cameras on our permanently carried mobile phones these days! What a great way to start being interested in and engaged with everyday surroundings!* [68]

Eventually, following your plan, without forcing the situation, you will be ready to make a commitment and become a dedicated wisdom-seeker or *'soul-smith'*, learning to identify and follow your unique, individual pathway to wisdom. This is the entry-point to 'Integration' Stage 5, during which a re-evaluation of one's values and behaviour from a universal perspective inevitably takes place, bringing one's life increasingly into line with the highest of altruistic ideals, growing naturally closer to others day by day, week by week, year by year.

Wisdom practices become increasingly second nature from here, as the authentic 'spiritual self' grows increasingly influential, while the force of the dissonant 'everyday ego' weakens. In addition, reassuring spiritual experiences (like those described in Chapter 2) are likely to grow increasingly

---

68. Heather Jane-James (2018) *Musings and a Few Unchallengeable Truths*, Amazon,pp 70-1.

powerful and frequent, confirming the wisdom path you now follow.

For many people, only a relatively small transition and re-orientation of priorities will be sufficient to move them firmly forward into Stage 5. Setting a sterling example (if barely noticed and often unheralded), such luminaries among us encourage others to do likewise in their turn, as the fruits of their spiritual practices shine forth, radiating out towards the community and further afield, creating and swelling incrementally a revitalised *World Wide Wave Of Wisdom*.[69] There may be resistance from some quarters, but there will also be plenty of encouragement. Embarking and persisting on this trail, discovering common ground with like-minded others, the thanks, praise and congratulations they receive in such supportive company serve to deepen each individual's commitment and promote further progress.

Later, without there necessarily being a noticeable crossing-point, we can expect a pristine (some would say 'newborn' or 'reborn') wisdom-seeker to emerge into 'Universal' Stage 6. To the wise, the length of time this takes will not be important, but others will want to know that progress towards full maturity takes a variable amount of time for different people, depending (with reference to Diagram 1 in Chapter 6) on the person's trajectory through the developmental stages – high, medium or low – and therefore the degree of dissonance that has built up between 'everyday ego' and 'spiritual self', which in turn will determine the amount of spiritual work remaining to be achieved.

In Stage 6, a seamless connection to the whole having been firmly grasped and fully accepted, many of the more persistent attachments and aversions are painlessly relinquished. Being, rather than doing or achieving, now takes priority. When

---

69. See Larry Culliford (2019) World Wide Wave of Wisdom, *Journal for the Study of Spirituality,* Vol 9. No1: 62-6. Also the 'World Wide Wave of Wisdom' website (See Appendix 2).

someone has realised – that is to say *made real* for herself or himself – life's *intrinsic* meaning in this way, they often appear to others both humble and saintly. This is the stage by which a person will have become a natural and spontaneous healer and teacher of others, living fully aware and present, in the moment, not preoccupied with sorry regrets for the past or anxious anticipation of the future. There is no fear of further loss, or even of death. You are home.

* * *

Reviewing the current state of humankind, afflicted as described at the beginning of the book with multiple inter-locking problems and sources of suffering, in thrall to dominant worldly, materialist values in capitalist democracies, the possibility of increasing numbers of individuals making progress on the spiritual path towards higher stages of wisdom and maturity offers significant hope for general well-being and a better, peaceful, safer, cleaner, healthier, much happier world.

Given the apparent rarity of spiritual teachers, an appeal to ordinary citizens becomes necessary, recommending greater degrees of spiritual awareness, the adoption of spiritual over worldly values, and at least some level of commitment to engaging regularly with the wisdom practices suggested.

Those associated with state authorities, religious organisations, large corporations, the media and other powerful agencies with a strong influence over public opinions, attitudes and behaviour will experience a significant opportunity, and may even feel a particular obligation, to review and alter their life priorities according to the guiding light of wisdom. The task involves working towards change, initially by instituting and encouraging discussion about the benefits of a spiritual worldview, championing a renewed primacy of spiritual over worldly values, and so rectifying the current dearth of wisdom in global society.

One notable change in recent decades, worthy of specific

attempts at reversal, has been the pressure on people's time to attend to their work and closely related matters. For example, research has shown that few people of working age currently get adequate sleep. (An average of between 7 and 9 hours per night is recommended by experts.) The need for sufficient rest and recreation cannot be given sufficient emphasis in the interests of boosting well-being and wisdom. A day filled with eight hours each of work, sleep, and relaxation, play and wisdom practices, plus a vital weekend day off to cultivate inner peace, outer harmony and fellowship, will also help and encourage people to prioritise and develop their PGPs and SDPs side by side.

As representing the future, children and adolescents are particularly worthy of consideration in the context of this discussion about the growth of wisdom worldwide. During Conditioning Stage 2 and Conformist Stage 3, young people are susceptible to major influences from family, teachers and the wider community that will also benefit from a thorough review.

A first priority would be to uncover, respect and allow boys' and girls' innate wisdom and personal character strengths to flourish. To support this aim, teaching meditation in schools is advisable and merits strong consideration, being a practice that will assist children to grow increasingly attracted to and infused with healthy patterns of politeness, respect for others, tolerance, kindness, honesty and other spiritual values. Such a practice will protect them against the emergence of a powerful, selfish 'everyday ego', and reduce to a minimum the risk of subsequent spiritual deficiency. Meditation, mindfulness or 'stilling' sessions held regularly in classes, even if relatively brief, will also help children maintain a valuable sense of mystery and a spirit of awe, wonder and delight in the subjects they are being taught, while they also learn the necessary facts and acquire the relevant skills. Teachers and parents, in the presence of emotionally well-balanced children, will benefit secondarily too. Furthermore, such wisdom behaviour as this undoubtedly begins a process that will be repeated more readily and advantageously generation by generation[70].

An aspect of childhood and adolescence that is often neglected, in a society where instant gratification is promoted in the interests of bolstering commerce, and where adults are too busy working to supervise adequately their young, concerns the importance of imposing firm restraint, sometimes called 'tough love'. By experiencing benevolent external restraint, a young person is much more likely to develop the kind of internal self-discipline that is of enormous benefit throughout life on the pathway to wisdom and maturity. It is not being mean or lacking generosity, for example, to withhold inessentials from a child (or from anyone else). This is being wise, even noble, as is firm encouragement in regard to manners, to saying 'please' and 'thank-you', for example, in maintaining personal hygiene, good social habits and personal dignity. Herein lies the antidote to many of the ills associated with today's youth, the many negative attitudes and behaviours that are spread through social media, which include bullying, suicidal behaviour, eating disorders, self-mutilation and so on. Good social habits taught by instruction are obviously better taught alongside consistent example from grown-ups.

As mentioned earlier (in Chapter 10), there may also be something to learn about the raising of young people from indigenous cultures. Native tribes benefit when their young people mature into adults through initiation programmes, a feature that is not replicated in western society. The rites of passage for both young men and women offer them the opportunity to face, experience and so come to master in particular the emotion of fear, and thereby to overcome the otherwise persistent drawback of self-doubt. To discover inner strength and courage in a time-honoured and sacred setting,

---

70. See footnote 56, also Noel Keating (2017) *Meditation with Children: A Resource for Teachers and Parents*. Dublin: Veritas Publications.

in this way, is of inestimable value, not only to the individual, but also to the community as a whole.

The Boy Scouts and Girl Guides movements, and the UK's Duke of Edinburgh Awards scheme, offer something comparable, as less formally do apprenticeships, university placements, Voluntary Service Overseas, the US Peace Corps, and military service. These are all commendable, as providing opportunities to develop self-discipline (while fostering various degrees of conformity or independence), while also leading to experiences of important, possibly challenging, differences through encountering different people and cultures, seeing how they live their lives. A 'gap year' period of work or travel offers a similar opportunity. There is plenty of scope in contemporary western culture to develop more satisfactory and better recognised rituals and rites of passage for young people, giving them the chance to develop maturity and wisdom, and earn the rewards of status and respect within society. At the same time, for the good of the whole, those many young citizens currently denied, or unsuited to, such opportunities are best not neglected. Viable growth opportunities are needed for as many young people as possible, especially the disadvantaged – those at high risk of poverty, educational deficiency, unemployment, delinquency, addictions, crime and imprisonment.

At the other end of the age scale, people who are old, ill, demented and dying require equally caring attention. The spiritual perspective insists that each person has a part to play throughout life until their final breath. It resolutely considers all the challenges presented by the elderly as opportunities. Faith in human compassion, courage and creativity may confidently be called upon to address and resolve difficult and distressing situations, large and small, as people continue to grow towards wisdom *through* pain and change, rather than by seeking to avoid them.

* * *

This book, incorporating findings from scientific enquiry together with observations derived through both logical and intuitive reasoning, is aimed primarily at prompting extensive, fruitful discussion on the subjects of wisdom, human suffering, spirituality and the path to maturity. A second principal aim is to provide a sound basis, guidance and encouragement for the many who may be inclined to investigate, deeply and personally, the universal mysteries and linked miracles of existence, life, consciousness, love and especially unity, by embarking upon a new start in life in search of wisdom: *the knowledge of how to be and behave for the best, for all concerned, in any given situation.* The wisdom journey begins with the realisation, deep down, that:

'We are all already one'.

* * *

Author's Notes

How *Seeking Wisdom* became *The Big Book of Wisdom*.

> **You may say that I'm a dreamer,**
> **but I'm not the only one.**
> **I hope someday you'll join us,**
> **and the world will be as one.** [71]

Occasionally an academic publication excites the attention of literary agents and mainstream publishers, eager to expand its previously limited circulation to a much wider readership, confident that it is sufficiently easy to follow and will bring value to many, many lives. That is the story of *Seeking Wisdom*, first published in 2017 by the University of Buckingham Press, and why it is being expanded, updated and re-issued by Legend in 2020 as *The Big Book of Wisdom*.

For an author, of course, this is thrilling. Confident all along that this book has exceptional qualities, I am delighted but not completely surprised. You see, in the summer of 2016 when my wife, Sarah, and I went on a holiday touring Scotland, having already written several books about spirituality, there did not seem to be anything more for me to say in that direction, but I was mistaken.

---

71. John Lennon (1971) Soundtrack of 'Imagine'.

We took the car ferry to the beautifully rugged, wild and windswept Isle of Mull, and the foot ferry as the sun broke through heavy clouds the following morning to Iona, to attend the Sunday morning service in the Abbey. The original community of monks arrived on this tiny island with St. Columba in the 6th century. From there they founded almost sixty churches, making it 'the cradle of Christianity in Scotland',[72] and from here, in the 7th century, St. Aidan travelled to initiate the famous monastery at Lindisfarne off the Northumbrian coast, an important moment in the spiritual history of the United Kingdom. The original Iona community was destroyed by Vikings in the year 802, but today's Iona Community, founded in 1938 by visionary minister, George MacLeod, is thriving.[73]

The restored Abbey church that morning was full. I do not remember much of the service, except beautiful music and a fairly traditional sermon about everyone having a unique type of spiritual work to do, the important first task being to discover what that is. I recall thinking, 'Yes, I've done that. Everything's fine. Mission accomplished so far!'

Afterwards, we went to the Visitor's Centre where, in the small 'books for sale' section, I was delighted to discover on the shelf two copies of my book *'Much Ado about Something'*, published two years earlier. Sometimes authors worry that nobody reads what we write, so this was a comforting experience, which might go some way to explaining why, that night back on Mull, I awoke at about 2.00 am with the title, chapter headings, and the entire outline for *'Seeking Wisdom'* perfectly clear in my mind. Sitting up and lighting the reading lamp, I hurriedly made notes in a bedside pad. Returning home a week later I immediately set to work, and the book was ready within a couple of months. The whole creative process had felt completely intuitive, natural and inspired.

---

72. See Appendix 2 for 'Welcome to Iona' website details.

73. See Appendix 2 for Iona Community website details.

It was a process that had its origins much earlier. After qualifying as a doctor and completing my 'house jobs' in 1975, I was not sure which branch of medicine to follow, so I decided to travel. I first took a six-month hospital job in New Zealand's North Island, and then looked for work in the South Island where, though, the options were limited, obliging me to accept a post in the Department of Psychiatry under Professor Ken Adam and Consultant Psychiatrist Max Bradfield. It was a training position, and by the time my New Zealand visa expired six months later, I had taken an important first step towards what would become my career; but I was not yet fully ready to embark upon it.

While in Christchurch, I managed to obtain a Residency Permit for Australia, and soon began a series of jobs covering a lengthy period, mainly as a locum doctor in general practice, working first in Tasmania, then New South Wales, Western Australia, and finally in South Australia. Eventually, I made a firm decision to resume psychiatry training, entering the training programme in the beautiful city of Adelaide; but this meandering, which lasted a couple of years, was a pivotal period for both my personal and professional development. With time often on my hands between jobs, I found myself reflecting on and trying to answer a simple question that had stayed with me since New Zealand: 'What is mental health at its best?' I felt certain that it was more than simply the absence of mental illness.

Building on the sciences of biology, chemistry and physics learned at school, we were taught from the first at medical school about healthy anatomy and physiology (the body's structure and how it works), before learning about pathology (what goes wrong) and therapeutics (how to fix it), then medicine, surgery, gynaecology etcetera. This was not the case in psychiatry training, where you might start, as I did, by learning about pathology, about depression and schizophrenia, phobias and obsessions, eating disorders and addictions, without any attempt to lay out for us a healthy overview of the subject.

I am a keen and well-trained scientist, but also felt intuitively that something vital was missing from the science-based, so-called 'medical model' that we were taught. It went like this: take a history (an account of the affected person's symptoms, also their life story, key relationships, and their habits), do a physical examination, examine the 'mental state' (a formal, text-book procedure), run some tests (such as blood tests, X-rays, scans and psychological tests), then make a diagnosis (name the disorder), and apply treatment... Bingo! But patients were human beings not machines, and psychiatric treatments often failed or were only partially successful, and were frequently accompanied by unpleasant side effects or frank toxicity.

Things have improved since the 1970s, I am happy to say. The medical model has been replaced by a more enlightened 'bio-psycho-social' model; but trainees are still not given, at the outset of training, any account of supreme mental health such as anyone might wish to attain, or of how to achieve it, yet this is what I was looking so carefully into and trying to pin down in words back in 1978 when I wrote my first book on the subject. I did so mainly for my own benefit, simply to make the complex subject as clear as possible for myself, and that book was never published; but some of the ideas have persisted with me, such as the need for a paradigm shift to include five dimensions – physical, biological, psychological, social *and* spiritual – to explain fully every aspect of human experience and understanding.

I am aware that, in a secular culture, there will be those who wish to challenge the idea of a real or actual spiritual realm, but this is not necessarily what is meant. People are asked only to accept that some individuals require and use legitimately the language of spirituality to describe experiences and events that occur to themselves and others, events of special power and significance that have the quality of mystery and are difficult to describe and explain in ordinary terms. Meaningful coincidences, which lead a person into thinking that an event or situation is 'meant to be', as if scripted by the cosmos, provide one common example. It is difficult to see how the reality or otherwise of a spiritual dimension can be proven scientifically beyond doubt, so it has therefore to be a question of personal experience. Those who seek it are obviously more likely to find it than those who do not.

A key idea attached to the five dimensions scheme, then, is that of 'spiritual awareness', a faculty or ability which people do well to cultivate on the road to what A Reza Arasteh has called 'Final Personality Integration',[74] in other words towards supreme personal well-being. This form of sensitivity involves a vital sense of being an integral part of a greater unity, of something altogether wholesome, awe-inspiring and grand; and this makes sense as a component of optimal mental health, because the experience of connection through this whole with everyone and everything else brings with it a calming and satisfying sense of belonging and self-worth. Spiritual or 'holistic'[75] awareness renders life increasingly meaningful, filled with purpose, and fosters enthusiasm for even the most mundane tasks of daily living.

Connection to the whole – to what from a spiritual perspective is, or appears to be, a divine or sacred unity – also proves, in this analysis, to be the source or origin of wisdom, associated as it is with values like honesty, humility and compassion, and attributes like imagination, intuition, creativity, and that immediate and empathic form of understanding and communication between self and others on which good relations between people depend. These capabilities must surely also be counted as aspects of supreme psychological health.

In terms of both mental illness and physical suffering, such

---

74. A Reza Arasteh (1975).

75. The word 'holistic' is related to both the words 'whole' and 'holy'.

a welcome, profound and seamless sense of connection is also beneficial through providing inner strength, courage and hope. Psychiatrists meet people daily in whom these attributes are lacking, people whose self-esteem has been damaged by their lives and their illnesses. How could mental health professionals, and health-care workers generally, not be interested and pay particular attention to this aspect of their patients' lives? That is a question still remaining to be answered. Furthermore, if this sense of connection is truly beneficial, how could such worthy people not also be interested in developing the same valuable faculty in their own lives? The practice of medicine, and particularly of psychiatry, offers a wonderful, if at times exacting, opportunity to learn and develop, to grow in both wisdom and compassion towards increasing spiritual maturity. In the final analysis, this is what drew me inexorably into the field, and has given me the greatest reward. It sometimes feels like psychiatry chose me, rather than the other way around.

I discovered from my patients, time and time again, that you can even have a highly destructive condition like schizophrenia and still, when the worst symptoms are in abeyance (either through natural remission or with the help of effective medication), have this kind of life-affirming experience. You can still feel a deep, calming and joyful spiritual connection to the universe, to everyone and everything in it. Until now, psychiatrists have tended to ignore and dismiss this, when their patients talk about it, as evidence of psychosis, of being 'out of touch with reality', and therefore part of the illness; but it is not so simple. Failing to assess the spiritual aspect of each person's condition, missing the healthy component, means failing also to help patients regain emotional strength and balance through it. This does them a genuine and regrettable disservice.

Here lies a paradox: a person can be sick in body and in mind while, at the same time, be healthy in spirit. Doubtless the reverse is also true. These are points I have found worth bearing in mind, together with the observation that sharing in suffering seems to bind people together with greater strength than does sharing pleasures. While the ability to remain still and silent is valuable, during meditation for example, I have observed that people grow mainly through adversity; their own and in sharing that of others, rather than by trying to evade pain and suffering. The American author, lecturer and political activist, Helen Keller, who was the first deaf-blind person to receive a university degree, is reported to have once said, *'Character cannot be developed in ease and quiet. Only through experience of trial and suffering can the soul be strengthened, vision cleared, ambition inspired, and success achieved.'* [76] Life is therefore much more fruitful when sickness, problems, losses, threats and other difficulties are faced squarely, than when people try so hard to avoid or circumvent them. Here is Helen Keller again: *'A happy life consists not in the absence, but in the mastery of hardships... The best way out is always through'.*

* * *

Getting back to the origins of the present volume, after writing that book in the 1970s, I continued with my enquiry into supreme mental health by looking into the question of distinguishing, if possible, human distress and anguish (such that anyone might experience in enormously challenging circumstances) from mental illness (as recognised by my profession). The lines are obviously blurred, but back then we were being taught that schizophrenia and major depressive illness often co-exist, failing to take full account of the probability that if a person suffered a major, debilitating psychotic episode in young adulthood, followed by continuing cognitive and emotional disability, the interruption of education, which resulted, accompanied by the inability to pass exams and obtain qualifications, get a well-paid job, or attract a life-partner,

---

76. See Appendix 2 for Helen Keller quotes website details.

would plunge anyone either into depression or (as was also common) into a state of rage; and that, alongside treating the psychiatric disorder, there was therefore healing work to be done, helping such a person meaningfully to grieve for what the illness had taken.

But my research also took me outside my professional work into the realms of wisdom and spirituality. I soon found that most of what I had discovered had been described and explained before. This is comforting for an independent researcher, to find themselves in harmony with other authorities, giving me the strongest sense that I was on the right track. It was also comforting that many wisdom teachers advise not blindly accepting what they say as true and useful; the important thing being to reflect on their advice and put it to the test for oneself.

Wisdom is universal, and as such is the subject of some of the oldest writings known to mankind. For example, I spent some profitable time in Australia with Tibetan Buddhist monks, who taught me the disciplined practice of meditation, which I have followed ever since. They also introduced me to the Buddha's teaching from 2,500 years ago, that human suffering begins with birth. If you have a body, it will hurt from time to time. If you have a mind, you will know emotional pain. Nobody escapes this. But the Buddha also said that there is a way to end one's suffering. Called, 'The Noble Eightfold Path', it is a manual of wisdom that, alongside my Christian upbringing, has influenced me considerably throughout life.

And that is something else I soon discovered, that wisdom is not the preserve of one religion. It is found at the heart of all the major world faith traditions and enlightened secular philosophies. Each has a distinct approach, and may seem very different from the others, but they all point towards the same central truths, like the many spokes of a wagon wheel holding the rim firm while pointing towards the central point of the axle. To navigate through and around the many problems religions can bring, as a result of their power to divide people, the time seems ripe now to be recasting wisdom in mainly secular language, and ally it as far as possible with the findings of contemporary science, to make it more fitting for the present times and contemporary culture. To this end, it seems appropriate and necessary to include in this book some important recent findings from neuro-science. Some questions, however, remain impenetrable to scientific methods of enquiry so that, where wisdom is concerned, a strong element of mystery will always persist. Attempts to avoid this conclusion, and thereby to get rid of doubt and ambiguity, must fail, and risk leading people astray. It has to be admitted that such attempts cannot be said to have gone particularly well for humankind so far.

In the 1600s, the philosopher Descartes announced *'I think, therefore I am'*, making rational thinking the basis of all certainty. Perhaps he only meant, *'I am conscious and aware'*, allowing for a kind of passive attentiveness to one's environment to confirm one's sense of existence, but the interpretation has always been since about reason, about thinking rationally; and the problem here is that logical, binary thinking tends to make the individual person central to his or her self-enclosed universe, seeing everything and everyone else as an object. As a continuing result, as the spiritual writer Thomas Merton has pointed out,[77] in our secular Western culture, we define ourselves by separating ourselves from other people, and have grown increasingly mechanistic and materialist, to the detriment of the world. Wisdom, involving recognition of our kinship to each other, is the opposite of this. We human beings are ultimately of one kind. Hence the value of kindness (*kind*-ness), and the need for a book like this, aimed at gently pulling everything back from discord towards social well-being, health and harmony.

'Seeking Wisdom' was originally sub-titled *'A Spiritual Manifesto'*. The reasons for this appear in the original

77. Thomas Merton (1988) *Thomas Merton in Alaska: The Alaskan Conferences, Journals, and Letters*. New York: New Directions. pp 131-2.

'Introduction'. The word 'manifesto' means, *'A public declaration of attitudes, aims and policies'*, so it was not entirely inappropriate. In the new version, however, although the book is still something of an extended declaration, the sub-title has been dropped, largely because it gave the impression that the book was mainly about the currently highly-contentious issue of politics (for which many people's appetite has understandably grown sated), whereas there is actually only one chapter concentrating on this subject.

A strong argument remains for the idea that, as the book originally declared, *'In order to thrive, a society needs recourse to language, values and practices associated with wisdom'*; but, foremost, this book is for people as individuals, not grouped together as 'society'. It is for people who will be able to affect and improve their communities by thinking, speaking and acting independently, gaining wisdom, and knowing how to behave well. The new, re-named version, *'The Big Book of Wisdom'*, is called 'Big', therefore, not because of a vast word count or enormous number of pages; far from it as you can see. It is 'Big' because wisdom is *for* everyone and *about* everything; in particular about everything connected to human welfare.

A new first chapter offers a brief definition of wisdom, gives reasons for seeking it, and addresses the urgency associated with a global culture and crowded planet facing significant and widespread problems resulting in extensive human suffering. This may seem like a dispiriting beginning, to be reminded of how much seems to be going wrong, but a good physician will always find it necessary to be clear about where the hurt lies, and to reflect on the underlying causes of pain and distress, before giving advice and offering remedies. Be assured, though, that the ultimate message here is one of hope; and part of that hope is to show how – both individually and together – everyone has the opportunity to play a meaningful part, working towards a better future.

Since completing my first book, I have continued writing

for my own benefit, mainly to work things out, get them as clear as possible in my mind, and so try to retain them in memory. Eventually, about twenty years ago, I began feeling an obligation to share my thoughts with others and so seek publication. I am not naturally a particularly humble person. The capacity for spending long periods in peaceful contemplation is matched, in my case, by also being irritable at times, impatient, even 'pushy'; wanting to get to the front, secure the best view, and all that. So I must state here that, rather than seeking praise or commendation, I make no personal claim for superior knowledge, ability, skill with words or anything, for such abilities can only land on someone as a kind of providential gift or blessing.

Furthermore, if I do have anything of value to say, it is on account of being a typical citizen like others, nobody special, and my claim concerns being, in so many ways, ordinary. This is particularly the case, for example, in terms of emotions. I am no stranger to worry, and am familiar with both anger and sadness in the face of imagined, threatened and actual losses. Equally, I know what it is like to feel calm, confident and happy when things are going well. If I am different in any way, if I have achieved a better level of emotional stability, of equanimity and resilience, than when younger; if, too, I live more fully in the present moment, not dwelling on the past or over-concerned with what may happen in the future, it is very likely connected with having made it my business to go looking for wisdom throughout a fairly long life, and anyone can do that. In truth, a major point of this book is to recommend exactly such a journey or quest.

The latest version of *The Big Book of Wisdom* in front of you now represents the culmination so far of my keen, earnest and ultimately joyful enquiry into the nature of supreme mental health. It cannot provide an infallible prescription, but it is aimed at providing encouragement and guidance for those readers who might wish, or even feel inwardly compelled, to embark upon or continue a similar search for everything that is true and wholesome, for spiritual knowledge and experience, as part of a kind of ongoing pilgrimage towards wisdom. Rather than thinking of the spiritual dimension of existence as a kind of specimen to pin down and dissect, it is more profitable to consider it as a wonderful adventure playground to explore, a place of excitement, fun and learning. It may feel threatening at times, but it is ultimately safe. Be assured that there can be no such thing as a wrong turn as you go; for every misstep provides, if nothing else, an opportunity to gain knowledge – about life and about oneself – to gain wisdom. And there is no need to rush.

That I have been inspired, in a way that seems uniquely special, leaves me inclined to trust that many will find these words ringing true, becoming for them an inspirational source not only of hope, but also of enthusiasm, courage and determination to face and grow through life's many challenges. *The Big Book of Wisdom* is meant to show as clearly as possible first *why* to go about such a noble endeavour, and then *how*.

Larry Culliford
World Mental Health Day
10th October, 2019

MORE ABOUT THE AUTHOR

 Dr Larry Culliford trained in medicine at St Catharine's College, Cambridge and Guy's Hospital, London. He worked in hospital medicine and general practice in UK, New Zealand and Australia, and later qualified as a psychiatrist, working until retirement in the UK National Health Service. Having published numerous books and articles on happiness, psychology and spirituality, his titles under the pen-name 'Patrick Whiteside' include:

The Little Book of Happiness (Rider Books, 1998 pb, & 2018 hb)
The Little Book of Bliss (Rider Books, 2000)
Happiness – the 30 day guide (Rider Books, 2001)[78]

Larry's titles under his own name include:

Love, Healing & Happiness (O Books, 2007)
The Psychology of Spirituality (Jessica Kingsley Publishers, 2011)
Much Ado about Something (SPCK, 2015)[79]

---

78. Personally endorsed by the Dalai Lama who said, "This book will be of benefit to many people".

79. Information about these books, which are all in print (except *The Little Book of Bliss)*, can be found on the author's website (see Appendix 2 for details).

Raised from childhood in the Anglican Christian tradition, Larry's religious development involved first leaving and some years later returning to Christian worship and practice. An independent and original thinker, having taken a close personal interest in many world faith traditions, he sometimes refers to himself as a 'universalist Christian', being thoughtfully open to the teachings and practices of both other religions and spiritually-minded secularist ideas and ideologies.

Dr Culliford was a co-founder in 1999 of the Royal College of Psychiatrists' *Spirituality and Psychiatry* special interest group. He is a former Chair of the Thomas Merton Society of Great Britain and Ireland and member of the International Thomas Merton Society. He is a long-term member of both the Scientific and Medical Network and the British Association for the Study of Spirituality (BASS), also a life-member of the Movement for the Abolition of War. [80]

Larry is married and lives happily in West Sussex, UK. No longer engaged in clinical practice, his activities include lecturing, also running occasional meditation and wisdom/spirituality workshops. He enjoys volunteering in a local primary school, and recently began learning to play the Spanish guitar. He has written a crime novel, *The Red Chairs Mystery* [81] featuring detective Holly Angel, whose next outing, *The Case of the Double Dutchman*, is in preparation. Larry has been happily addicted to playing golf since childhood. When once asked what he was best at, he said, *"Sleep... If it was an Olympic sport, I could sleep for my country"*. As you can *Imagine*, that makes him a pretty good dreamer too.

* * *

---

80. See Appendix 2 for website details of these organisations.

81. Published by Troubador in 2019. See Appendix 2, under 'Author's crime novel', for details.

Appendix 1: References and Recommended Reading

Alcoholics Anonymous (2001) *Alcoholics Anonymous, 4th Edition*, New York: Alcoholics Anonymous World Services Inc.

A. Reza Arasteh (1975) *Toward Final Personality Integration: A Measure for Health, Social Change, and Leadership*, 2nd edition. New York and London: Wiley.

Thomas Byrom (1976) translator. *The Dhammapada: The Sayings of the Buddha*. London: Rider Books.

Jonathan Campion & Sharn Rocco (2009), 'Minding the Mind: The Effects and Potential of a School-Based Meditation Programme for Mental Health Promotion', in *Advances in School Mental Health Promotion*, Vol 2:1

Larry Culliford (2007) 'Taking a Spiritual History', *Advances in Psychiatric Treatment*, 13:3

Larry Culliford (2009) 'Teaching Spirituality and Health Care to Third Year Medical Students', *The Clinical Teacher*, 6:1.

Larry Culliford (2011) *The Psychology of Spirituality: an introduction*, London: Jessica Kingsley Publishers.

Larry Culliford (2015) *Much Ado About Something: a vision of Christian maturity,* London: SPCK.

Larry Culliford (2019) 'World Wide Wave of Wisdom', *Journal for the Study of Spirituality,* Vol 9. No1: 62-6.

Erica M Elliott (2019) *Medicine and Miracles in the High Desert: My Life among the Navajo People.* Bloomington, Indiana: Balboa Press.

David Hay & Rebecca Nye (2006) *The Spirit of the Child* (Revised Edition). London: Jessica Kingsley Publishers.

David Hay (2006) *Something There: The Biology of the Human Spirit.* London: Darton, Longman and Todd Ltd.

Heather Jane-James (2018) *Musings and a Few Unchallenge-able Truths,* Amazon.

Noel Keating (2017) *Meditation with Children: A Resource for Teachers and Parents.* Dublin: Veritas Publications.

Dalai Lama & Desmond Tutu with Douglas Abrams. (2016) *The Book of Joy: lasting happiness in a changing world.* London: Hutchinson.

David Lorimer (2017) *Survival? Death as a Transition.* Hove: White Crow Books, pp 209-10.

Iain McGilchrist (2009) *The Master and his Emissary: The Divided Brain and the Making of the Western World.* New Haven and London: Yale University Press.

Tom McLeish (2018) *The Poetry and Music of Science.* Oxford: Oxford University Press.

Linda Mercadante (2014) *Belief without Borders: Inside the Minds of the Spiritual but not Religious*. New York: Oxford University Press.

Thomas Merton (1948) *The Seven Storey Mountain*, New York: Harcourt, Brace & company.

Thomas Merton (1966) *Conjectures of a Guilty Bystander*. New York: Doubleday & Company, Inc.

Thomas Merton (1973) *The Asian Journal of Thomas Merton*. New York: New Directions.

Thomas Merton (1988) *Thomas Merton in Alaska: The Alaskan Conferences, Journals, and Letters*. New York: New Directions.

Thomas Merton (2008) *Thomas Merton: A LIfe in Letters - the essential collection*, selected and edited by William Shannon and Christine Bochen. New York: Harper Collins.

Kent Nerburn (2017) *Neither Wolf Nor Dog: on forgotten roads with an Indian Elde.*, Edinburgh: Canongate.

Barack Obama (2008) *Dreams from my Father*. London: Canongate.

Geshe Rabten, Geshe Ngawang Dhargyey (1977) *Advice from a Spiritual Friend*. New Delhi: Publications for Wisdom Culture.

Dean Radin (1997) *The Conscious Universe: the scientific truth of psychic phenomena*. San Francisco: HarperEdge.

Monika Renz (2015) *Dying: a transition*. New York: Columbia University Press.

Monika Renz (2016) *Hope and Grace: spiritual experiences in severe distress, illness and dying*. Jessica Kingsley Publishers.

Richard Rohr (2012), *Falling Upward: a spirituality for the two halves of life*. London: SPCK.

Michael Shearer (2014) *Walking a Rainbow*. CreateSpace, Amazon.

Victor Schermer (2003) *Spirit and Psyche: a new paradigm for psychology, psychoanalysis and psychotherapy*. London and New York, Jessica Kingsley Publishers.

Steve Taylor (2011) *Out of the Darkness: From turmoil to transformation*. London: Hay House.

Steve Taylor (2018) *Spiritual Science: why science needs spirituality to make sense of the world*. London: Watkins.

Greta Thunberg (2019) *No One Is Too Small To Make A Difference*. London: Penguin/Random House.

Appendix 2: Websites

The Abbey of Our Lady of Gethsemani: www.merton.org
accessed 11th September 2019.

Author's blog: www.psychologytoday.com/gb/blog/
spiritual-wisdom-secular-times
accessed 14th October 2019.

Author's website: www.ldc52.co.uk
accessed 14th October 2019.

Author's crime novel: www.troubador.co.uk/bookshop/
crime-and-thrillers/the-red-chairs-mystery
accessed 14th October 2019.

BASS, The British Association for the Study of Spirituality:
www.basspirituality.org.uk
accessed 14th October 2019.

Brahma Kumaris (World Spiritual University) UK:
www.brahmakumaris.uk
accessed 16th October 2019.

Extinction Rebellion: www.rebellion.earth
accessed 20th August 2019.

The Galileo Commission: www.galileocommission.org
accessed 2nd September 2019.

Gandhi quotes: www.goalcast.com/2017/03/20/top-20-inspiring-mahatma-gandhi-quotes/
accessed 14th September 2019.

Helen Keller quotes: www.goalcast.com/2017/05/05/top-helen-keller-quotes-inspire-you-never-give-up
accessed 14th October 2019.

The Iona Community: www.iona.org.uk/about-us/history
accessed 8th August 2019.

The Institute of Noetic Sciences: www.noetic.org/about/origins
accessed 11th September 2019.

The Thomas Merton Center and The International Thomas
Merton Society (ITMS): www.merton.org
accessed 14th October 2019.

The Thomas Merton Society of Great Britain and Ireland:
www.thomasmertonsociety.org.uk
accessed 14th October 2019.

Meditation in Schools (MindSpace):
www.meditationinschools.org
accessed 12th October 2019.

Mindfulness in Schools Project: www.mindfulnessinschools.org
accessed 12th October 2019.

'One Strange Rock' documentary, episode 10; National Geographic:
www.youtube.com/watch?v=XrC4vDcWmxk&list=
PL0Bj4UPMqsHAcOUxGBYxjkiVjgJiDuGLl
accessed 11th September 2019.

The Royal College of Psychiatrists' *Spirituality and Psychiatry* Special Interest Group:
www.rcpsych.ac.uk/members/special-interest-groups/spirituality
accessed 12th October 2019.

The Religious Experience Research Centre:
www.uwtsd.ac.uk/library/alister-hardy-religious-experience-research-centre
accessed 26th August 2019

The Scientific and Medical Network:
www.explore.scimednet.org
accessed 14th October 2019.

The St Barnabas Hospice 'schools project':
www.stbarnabas-hospice.org.uk/our-care/hospice-schools-project
accessed 12th October 2019.

Welcome to Iona: www.welcometoiona.com
accessed 12th October 2019.

World Wide Wave of Wisdom: www.wwwow.net
accessed 2nd October 2019.

* * *